THE MORNING SONG OF LORD ZERO

poems old and new

CONRAD AIKEN

The Morning Song
of Lord Zero

NEW YORK   OXFORD UNIVERSITY PRESS
1963

Copyright 1944, 1945, 1946, 1947, 1948, 1949, 1952, 1955,
©1958, 1959, 1960, 1961, 1962, 1963 by Conrad Aiken
'A Letter from the Grass' and 'Count the Summer'
Copyright ©1963 by The Curtis Publishing Company
Library of Congress Catalogue Number 63-11915

Some of the poems in this book first appeared in the following
publications: *The Atlantic Monthly, The Georgia Review, Harper's Bazaar,
New Republic, Pacific, Poetry, Ramparts: The National Catholic Journal,
Show, Saturday Review, The Virginia Quarterly Review,* and *Wake.*

Permission to include 'The Cicada,' 'Aubade,' 'The Accomplices,'
'The Meeting Place,' 'The Fluteplayer,' 'Herman Melville,'
'When You Are Not Surprised,' 'Portrait,' 'The Fountain,' and
'The Cyclades' has been granted by Thomas Yoseloff, The Sagamore Press.

Printed in the United States of America

contents

one

THE MORNING SONG OF LORD ZERO

Gambler and spendthrift by nature
chameleon soul whose name is Zero
anonymous in headlines
nameless in breadlines
nevertheless I am your hero.
Today an upstart millionaire from Mozambique
polyglot but sans Latin and sans Greek
très debonair très chic
I am inscrutably someone else tomorrow
when I speak
all languages at will:
the cashier's till
spills me a quicksilver word
the gilded shill
coos me another
I am your jack-and-jill
of all trades dubious brother
panhandler father Cassandra mother
and yet in the end insidiously
o indispensably and invidiously
something more.
Watch me sneak from door to door:
with tongue in cheek
but ready with the o so adaptable speech
I knock on each:
listen to my sales-talk: love, and honor,
courage, cowardice, virtue, vice,
belief and disbelief!

3

Down the immortal and dreadful street
where man your image extends himself forever
I your Greek-gift-bearing donor
I, but believe me! your Cassandra
knock and knock
(do not call me vox et praeterea nihil)
and if no answer
stoop and try the lock
hoping still to find
somewhere some day
the sacred and vulgar key
to you or me.

                              Azrael pass thou not by
                              shade not today this tree.

I am he
and this I share with you
in this perhaps alone am true
who cannot infringe upon cannot conceive
the arcane process by which he might believe
or not believe or learn or know
begin or not begin choose or not choose: who came
without a name
as also without intention: knows no measure
save only that with which the umbilical cord
provided him *tout court* of pain or pleasure:
rising not with the sun
but the day well begun
to brush his teeth and defaecate and eat
innocently sans knowledge of their meanings
or of his own:
and thus goes forth to face the preposterous unknown.
Can you remember what I remember?
Are we of one substance? Are we flesh or stone?
Yet brought by solar synthesis together
comedians of the soul's capricious weather
obedient to who-knows-what

we seek to chart
disturbances of the heart
goblin manifestations of All Souls' November
the golden monstrances of May.
I your hero take apart
in layered laminae the infinite platitude
figure degrees of magnitude
in man's imagination
of which the application remains obscure
pick up with tweezers some idiot surd of meaning
so summoning the morning stars to shout together
and thus with gradual decimals construct
the glass-topped hearse
that is our universe.

Belly to belly and skin to skin
O lift the latch and come right in
will you have me now or will you hesitate?
We played pinochle and we stayed out late
ate fish and chips at the Golden Gate
then crumpled the morning papers.
Know what the well-primed critics say
of pseudo-Shakspere's latest play
tragedy or farce or melodrama
witness the sad strip-tease
of Lesbian lads and Panic lasses
forgotten as soon as seen.
Take the express to Bowling Green
and watch the rosy-fingered dawn
practicing her matutinal flattery
above the Battery
then tip out one by one the firefly lights
and change to a golden crab the Staten Island ferry.
Brief is our measure, let us be merry.

Look love the miracle is with us it is the body
the holy dwelling the acceptable machine
our own divine composing room
provided for us from the womb
alive and with its own precipitate and unpredictable aliveness
prismatic vision of the world no less
so brilliant that unless we blink
or do not stop to think
eyes and mind
are both struck blind.
How in this whole magnificence to find
our own self-seeking and self-shaping phrase
and so ordain our days?
Lord how the streets now shine
as the Great Opiate's eastern conduits run with wine
and pour into the sea. Dull would we be
if we withheld the attribute divine
from brick and stone and flesh
and from the awakening and self-breathing tree
the tree of heaven
spellbound in its epiphany
as the proud clocks strike seven.

And the intricacies begin:
without, within,
holy observed and holy observing
leaf adoring tree and tree admiring leaf
shape loving shapelessness and shapelessness shape
as unbelief worships belief!
See how the light shines through
the vascular leaf
green veins with gold shot through:
how we are of star's light made
and now distinct in sun and shade
of bloodstream made
and sunstream made.

Look through your hand and see
the blood against the sun
look into the sea
o mother mother
where with our fanlike fins
mind begins
and intricacy begins:
with what sacred and secret separations
and with what love
we are made to move!
Lightly now softly now
inward now outward now
frowardness and towardness now
dance and chance, as
intricacy begins
and again begins!
Song is our study
this is our body
see how the leaf comes
as out of death come
fresh the belief comes
and time begins!
Here on this hill
we number the possible
resume the acceptable
and intricacies begin!
Sunshape and earthshape
manshape and deathshape
wormshape in sunflower
godshape in dream.

Smith is early today and Jones is late
the box-trees by the Funeral Home have been watered
the newspaper truck throbs by the news-stand at the corner
the Shamrock Grill is open turnstiles are clacking
the cobbler in the window of Shoes Rebuilt
peers down at the heel he is tacking

the green light says Walk the red light says Stop
take me quick to the apothecary shop
we dial Meridian for the split jewel of time
and Weather for the windsong of weather.
Who needs a change of scene
walks with the green
into the unfolding world
himself too unfolding
the stage is struck the lights change
the street grows strange
it leads without hesitation forever
into our own involuntary invention
among the whispers and rainbows
of the unexpected
the fairyland
that waits to be named
between life and death.

    Azrael Azrael
    winged with thunder
    pass thou not by this day
    let no thing die
    the farmer sun is hastening
    the western hill is glistening
    the eastern honeycombs are filled
    with crocus light
    it is farewell to night
    see that this day no thing be killed.

    But if thy daily dead
    old thunder head
    thou yet must have then take instead
    the bee's faint shadow on the hill
    but the bee spare and daffodil
    leave all else living still
    under the opening eyelid of the sky
    swoop thou not hawklike by.

X iii

Who are you? Who?
Fatigue this might be, or repetition
as the shutter drips sunshine in a known pattern,
bright drops falling
in a water-chain of light. The dream
hangs from the morning ceiling like a canopy,
illusory mosquito-net in whose folds
our old terror again insinuates itself to hide:

but no: it is not repetition nor fatigue
nor the prospect of sameness nor apprehension of change:
the footstep shifts to left or right
among crossed grassblades by the broken spout
to the galaxy of pebbles you call a path:
nor is it only the differing heartbeat
which hums in your heart as you go forth to discover:

the hum of the heartbeat linking past and future
as sun binds with gold the leaves in the tree
for the moment of sharing in which you partake
as Socrates lifts his cruse of hemlock:
acceptance and question in a single libation
celebration and farewell in a final gesture
the first and last taking of the breast:

at every instant of the perpetual intersection
of one with another in bloodstream and firmament
you are again born and again die
only O Phoenix to arise again in flame
immutable mutable of sunlight
again dripping from the shutter
and humming in the heart for another morning:

Jesus still walking down the galaxy of pebbles
to divide order from disorder

9

Blake sucking the wound in Achilles' heel
while the thorn-scratch festers on your ankle
and squirrel kisses squirrel on the bough of balsam:
as moment indivisibly and invisibly creates moment
and you walk from yourself into yourself.

The landscape why is it not as we had foreseen it
there are hills before us but no mountains
and a river winding behind the hills
and see on the hills the blessed creatures
lions composed and unrampant under a flight of birds
in a ladder of light
and there in one corner a last pocket of night
ravelling away to the sun.
The waterfalls are not exactly those of the mind
dropping their blue against the green
it is all familiar but also unfamiliar
known and unknown true and untrue
benign but also perilous
and as we step into the meadow
we feel the shadow that is not precisely a shadow
the breath that is not precisely a breath. Death
surely has not preceded our footsteps here
surely does not follow us? The landscape
opens unhesitatingly before us
hills from rivers roll back
pathways open to left and right
our feet are now in the morning brook
and its clear parable of time
the tree is under our hands and over our heads
and as we move to what we do not know
and can never rightly imagine
all these become the ambiguous language
by which we come to pass
and learn to see
and mean
and be.

THE PHOENIX IN THE GARDEN

The Garden

Silence. The hour of the Phoenix.
And who is waiting, if not ourselves,
for another of the bland sequences of twilight,
that most ambiguous of transformations. We observe
the subtle succession, so innocent, so seemingly unprepared,
from one color to another, from shade to lesser shade,
and thus by degrees to the absolute. But it is not
ourselves alone who are involved: no such thing.
No, not projected by those who dream, far less
by us, who have no meaning, the lawn
(forgive me) is not emerald, nor orient jade, and lately tarnished
by the seasonal trades. Heavy July
has emptied the birds' nests. The frogs
sulk in the pool, diminuendo.
And the ancient trees, our sad acacias,
those dirty trees, the gardener calls them,
forever littering, scattering —

The Streetlamp

Speak for yourself, old garden,
but not for me. Only at nightfall
I light that secret stage of yours:
am but a candle-holder, who, after dark,
will serve to trace, for a serpent's-tongue flicker of time,
the broken curve of an arch

11

or empty an urn of shadow
or expose the brute flank, lichened marble,
of goat-god Pan. Understanding nothing,
remembering nothing. But you
and all your perjured altars—

The Garden

So you might say: and that crude light of yours
a vulgar penetration. Turn away
the indifferent and infertile eye,
that once more I might wonder
why you are you and I am I
and why
together forked in such conjunction,
base gerundive of nature. As if—as if—
But now the clock strikes. Now begin—
Phoenix!—and welcome in
the unwelcome strangers.

The Phoenix

                                        I cry I cry

human shape not human
trees not arboreal the terrestrial earth
not plausible earth and my wings not wings
but flames that flake and fall and as they fall
consume us all
I cry I cry

The Garden

And so it comes again, winter and summer
sun or rain it comes again.
The rake is not as cruel with the leaf
as between new-met lovers disbelief.
And sod, upturned, discloses,
the agonizing roots of roses.
                                        And here they come.

The Man
Perfection, it may be—or imperfection it may be—

The Woman
Or confection perhaps. What a delicious garden. The leaves
are not of the fig, nor figment, one believes
in neither. And with what grief conceives
of that pained love, suffocating and insufferable,
the eyes lowered, blinded, the tranquil house
where dwells the spirit
blown in, blown out, by the wind of desire, diswindowed
of time and place!
                          Yet one can wind one's hair
—look now—upon this broken stair
or round a pinchbeck pin
o god as if it were a world
and not have back a word.
                          Garden, garden,
why do we walk here, stand here? And poor man
why flown together?

The Phoenix
I cry I cry
not flown not flown disown
that word of wings how can you own
human shape not human
embodiment of air and mind together
and so sail off like me in any weather
flame I come and flame I go—

The Man
I know. And I know more. I know
what the leaf thinks in the pregnant garden, green inscription
decipherable only to the tree and root
and the eventual seed and the inevitable fruit
and yes poor woman
in all that here compels us.

13

The Woman
Ophidian and recondite comes the demon.

The Garden
Look—they have been petrified in the very act
the extreme act
of prayer.

The Streetlamp
Hair twined with hair beneath my Gorgon stare.

The Phoenix
I cry and shall cry again
human shape not human
man not man woman not woman
man not woman nor woman man since time began
the ashes sing beneath my wing.

The Streetlamp
I am a candle-holder, I am patient.
And who knows which most matters, that which happens
or what's in darkness or in light—this garden
and the two strangers and the stranger Phoenix
and all these shuttlings through the shutter of light.
Let them be blest, if blest they can be, by my light.

THE OLD MAN AND THE SHADOW

The Old Man
Perils of daybreak and the sharp shutters of light,
and you here once again my ancient familiar,
old chameleon, protean ghost:
you down there in the corner of my heart
or abroad in the wilderness of morning
but as always without dimension:
                              Tiny as a caraway seed
or sudden as a tree of lightning
or ingenuous as a cloud in summer.
                              I have watched you sliding
down the black windowpane in a make-believe of rain:
in the hollow of midnight I have heard you
whining like the wind through a crack in the door.
                              Old hieroglyph!
Your name is written indelibly in the innocence of light:
innumerable and ingenious have been your disguises:
but in the end I always unmask you:
and in the end I am always afraid.

The Shadow
It is yourself of whom you are afraid, Old Man,
it is not I.

The Old Man

Once I found you hiding in the palm of my hand.
And once at high noon in my own mirrored eye,
a pinpoint of something unknown and invidious
opening subtly as a little shutter into darkness,
to divulge, at the far end of an interior corridor,
that shape which you will never quite confess to.
       I have felt you hurrying
close behind me in the golden folds of the sunlight
inaudible and invisible footsteps
mischievously following and mocking my own.
Perhaps we were born together, are inseparable?
But no matter what your name is, I am afraid.

The Shadow

I am the accompaniment, Old Man, you the tune.
But am I not also your invention?
You are the object, I the shadow.
How then can you be afraid?

The Old Man

Many and diverse have been my studies: of the far and near,
the simple, the recondite, the fabulous, the remote in time,
of abstract theorem and sober particular practice,
of assumed divine and presumed profane.
I have tested like the intrepid and intelligent spider
the webs and calligraphies of the geometer
and those no less diaphanous
of vertebrate and invertebrate verse.
I have considered the intense anatomies of man and mind
and their solubility in the mortal but godlike body
as at last in the understanding of understanding
and the dissolution of the word.
But always inevitably step by step with my study
pari passu pari passu
I have been aware of an accompanying footfall
and an interior purpose and an interior voice.

It is you who introduce the metrical pauses
that give meaning to the far, slow, almost silent song
of the wood thrush hidden in the pinewood
like love concealed in the heart.
                              It is you
who set an end to the song an end to the love
and bring the theorem no matter how perfect
to a silent conclusion. And I am afraid.

        The Shadow
Dismiss me as merely an echo, Old Man,
as perhaps only the slight sound of your own time
your own little machine running down in time.
                              Embrace me
as you would yourself. How then can you be afraid.

        The Old Man
Measure is of no avail in this ulterior kingdom.
Not the pure rondures of simplicity
nor the all-seining nets of subtlety
no nor the arcane notations of the wizard bloodstream
no more than the clear modes of the mountain brook
can here be valid. Flux cannot measure flux.
The partitions and precisions of the caliper
no more endure than the scansions of the verse
as the verse no more endures than the voice.
The intrusion is yours. And I am afraid.

        The Shadow
Perhaps we are functions, one of the other? A conceit of light?

The Old Man

Yes, it is true, you were always the intruder.
But nevertheless how can we speak of intrusion?
For which comes first, the light or the shadow?
And who am I to pretend to be light?
Together conceived, together created in synthesis,
shadow conspiring with light and light with shadow,
the rose a promise in the invisible
and the invisible a premise of the rose:
must we accept this duplicity? Is this our conclusion?
If so, I am afraid.

The Shadow

If you are afraid, Old Man, then fear is inborn:
initial: a part of yourself: as I am you.
Change, I change with you: move, I move:
vanish, I vanish. But there is nothing, no, no, nothing,
that I can add or subtract. Not now, not ever.

The Old Man

The decimals betray it! and the mortal clocks
that appraise and applaud the sun! the moons of the fingernail
declare it and the frost on the sweetfern
and the tide that recedes and the tide that returns
and the galaxies in flight with their seasons.
                          The wildflowers
danced on a wave of light to make time and place for man
and will again be gone with the dark.
                          Here in my hand
like an ignorant palmist I read
the salt histories of hunger and love
recorded in a whisper of dust that drew breath
to become myself. Let us at last admit it.
Death is born with us. And I am afraid.

LANDSCAPE WITH FIGURES

Lizard under leaf and the eye gold
the moment motionless the morning silent
spider motionless in spangled web
while the fly buzzes and considers

and then twig falls on silent moss
o as the moment loosens in a dream
image of tree from image of love
or an old hatred from a known face

see how the landscape recedes outward and inward
and is peopled like an old painting with desires
the morning-glory opening its purple sex to the bee
who hums off to the geometric hive

while near at hand the cow crops while bull couples
and children in the swing tell tales
of lewd fathers and aunts in an attic
and pussy drowned in a well

the sun is upended by the turning earth
old lechers that they are in time and turning
plough slants athwart the light and oakleaf too
and the raw furrow shines

and song and song from the woods
o song o song from what does it come
is it there outside from the birds on the hill
or from the inner landscape which is I

birds landscape trees and bees and I
and the cows coupling and the morning-glory
seducing the mind's bee for the mind's crystal hive
all's bloomed and blessed at once

even to the shadow pencilled from the burning bush
which surely points to nightfall
where bee like heart sleeps in the image of death
and landscape inner and outer are again still.

INCIPIT FINIS FINIS INCIPIT

Morning comes, and with renewed devotion.
The dragons and angels of sleep
whirl up our dreams about them and dislimn,
fade far away into the daybreak ocean,
lost in the music of the waking mind,
sans signature. And now the blind
pathway unwinds from inward to outward,
while from the outer world roars sunrise in.

The bird sings sings sings sings
but who can tell
whether from the heart rings that slow bell
or in the eye or on the tongue
outside or inside outdoors or in
still in the dream we hear it begin
telling of break of day or break of heart.

What did we sleep for and why wake?
Who was it made us, and why make?
And who began this lordly give-and-take?
Look, children, rise,
and stroke the cobwebs from your eyes,
the innocence and violence pour in
as day begins
and we begin—

—just where we started from. But where
where where where did we start,
what god invented heart
or the sure stream from heart to hand
from wild sea to wild land
where the bird sings sings sings
into our haunted waking
and thought begins its taking?

This we shall never know,
old ocean-flow from long ago.
Evening, and we shall reach
our ending on that beach
starfish stranded on sand
waiting for morning and renewed devotion
and from the ocean
another dream reaching its curious hand.

A LETTER FROM THE GRASS

Indeed, child, the little pimpernel, most modest
and obscure of flowers, which here you see
between the tree-roots, the tiny star
of dusty red, or is it vermilion, each petal
with a most delicate point, and the clouded center,
and, yes, like something one might discover
coming through the far eye of a telescope
on a blue night in summer—indeed this little flower
will speak to us if we will listen.
                                        It will say

something of the noiseless unfolding of the shutters of daybreak
in the great silence of morning, something too
of the manifold infoldings of nightfall: it will praise
with its own voice, its own small voice, but no less clear
or dear for that, the infinitesimal
tickling and tinklings of its beginnings,
when the pale root-foot breaks the seed
to adventure downward into darkness, while the pale stalk,
longing to be green, to be green, yearns itself upward
to salute with its new hands the sun.
                                        It will say

that life is whole, although it be but for a day
of one's own circling with the circling world
until the shut-eye planets bid us to sleep.
One day, and we have learned it all,
from the first feathered shadow's fall,
whether from tree or garden wall,
until once more the invisible ladder
of sunlight climbs to noon. And so revolving,
and so returning with our praise, until that time
when again shadows with the dead moon climb.
Now its eye opens, then it will close.
And this is what it knows.

COUNT THE SUMMER

Count the summer with your fingers, the minutes fly
from foxglove bell to resinous cone, and it may be
the last of all to come. The song-sparrow
forgets his song, sings only half of it,
and that half-heartedly. Who fears to die,
dies with the fearing
who cares to live
lives in the caring.

Mention the names and with the mention
foxglove and sticky cone and wide-eyed brier
and the seconds of the fountain bright
as falling light
these will become the unsure pulse in the wrist
your love-in-the-mist
the spider's one and only web-caught amethyst
your own invention.

Old heart of self regard your secret weather
in the interstices of leaf and southwest wind
hold up your hand
to see the blood in it against the sun
where now you run
as runs your own self-measuring time.
Caught in this self-wrought and unfinished rhyme
you and the world perish together.

25

MORNING DIALOGUE

The Young Man
That way the moonflower and the sunflower this
and the garden path that winds between
how can I know what they may mean
in the confusions of my delight?
       Old mother oak
whose ferrule is on my forehead
whose mast is on my tongue
tell me, for I am young,
what language I should speak?

The Oak
Speak with the language of the leaf
when what you mean is brief
and with the language of the bough
when what you mean is more than now
but also learn while you are young
speech is not only of the tongue.

The Young Man
This calyx of cerulean blue
now magnified by one clear drop of dew
becomes tremendous in the sun
and every one
of these small dots of cinnamon
seems like a world about to run
into the fiery histories of space
how can I face
these miracles and have no speech?

The Oak

                    I reach
from earth to sky, from one to other,
have no sister and no brother
from the dark underworld
crammed with richness and with death
seek out my way to leaf and breath.

The Young Man

What love is this
that can dispense with words
or all but such as bud and fade and fall
heedless of the song of birds
once more to earth that buries?

The Oak

North wind begins his autumn flurries
a solitary leaf descends
and something ends.
You too must die
and so must I
yet each with different speech can say—

The Young Man

                    —What can we say?

The Oak

I have forgotten. Something simple—?
That night is night, and day is day.
Or that the languages of sap and blood
are only wood and word
and therefor good.

THREE VOICES AT THE MERIDIAN

The Cat

Noon, and its excellent sun, and you, old tree,
and here squat I, heraldic and sejant in sequined shadow,
and the same question taunts us as before,
which is the older? cat or tree? you or me?
The houses with their hands before their eyes
the shuttered houses they are younger surely?
And the pale nuns who pace demurely
under the purple Judas bloom?
But which is the older, you or me?
                    And you, old tomb!
freezing in the shadow, sweating in the sun!
tell us again which is the oldest of us three?
I walk and talk I walk and sleep
my own concerns and seasons keep,
then, twilight come,
put on that evil which is second nature
to every living creature.

The Tree

Nothing is older nothing is evil
thus to question is to invite the devil
by man called conscience or else consciousness
in his unenviable and self-created doom
invented out of time and out of mind
that he might call himself mankind
and who knows why.

                    Better the acorn
dropped for the dark-eyed squirrel to carry and bury
better the bitter berry
for the quail's green crop.
                    Better the drop
of wild honey or innocent rain
than this all-man-invented pain.

        The Man
Latecomer that I am, old cat, old tree, old tomb,
yet grant me room. Ungainly I
the body awkward and unshod and shoddy
what mind indeed would choose such body
dropped from the bloody womb
the spirit shy?
                    Yet I
count time and make it rhyme
and know the reasons
for your seasons.

SNAPPED STRING, BROKEN TREE

Never gainsay death
you who visibly die
who shrink from the wind
or the shadow of a wing
and know in the beat of the heart
the shape of things to come
yourself the bare oak
when the north wind whistles
yourself the snapped string
when the music stops.

Stay yourself with icicles
lie down in the new grave
and shroud yourself with rose-petals
or warm yourself with an *ignis ossium*
to dance the rites of spring
you are still the bare oak
motionless in snow
still the snapped string
when the music stops.

And who would ever wish
to gainsay goodfellow death
whose embrace is Judas blossom
whose eye is apple blossom
whose footfall is the sure silence
between tick and tock
who would wish to gainsay
night after day
end after beginning?

The shadow of the oak
becomes a map in the mind
and moves in the mind
on the winds of the mind
and every movement of it
becomes a new word
and every word becomes a new leaf
yourself the bare oak
listening to spring
yourself the tuned string
touched to sing.

ONEIROMACHIA

We are the necromancers who once more
magically make visible the night
recapture that obscure obscene delight
fathom its undertow and in one net
fish up foul fables we must not forget
have them alive and slippery in our hands:
what are we but divided selves that move
to find in all that glittering thrash our love?

We'll summon in one dream all motives forth
and you shall be the south and I the north
and we will speak that language of the brain
that's half of Portugal or all of Spain
or of those yet unsounded seas
that westward spawn beneath the menstrual moon:
what are we but divided souls that live
or strive to in the sundered self of love?

Splinter the light and it will dream a rainbow
loosen the rainbow and it will stream in light
divide the brightness and you'll build a wall.
But we'll a twilight be, a go-between
of midnight and of daybreak, and beget
marvels and monsters we must not forget:
these are the language that love dared not speak
without which we can neither make nor break.

WAKING IN THE MORNING

And so, with the ear pressed hard to the pillow,
and the heart held downward, and downward its beating,
the light teasing now at the closed eyes of shutters
as the wild dreams tease at the doors of the mind,
we arrive, old body, old heart, and old mind,
at yet, yet another ambiguous answer,
but perhaps just sufficient with which to begin.

The cat's-cradle wheatstalks become a cloud castle
and the castle a ghost-laden hawsehole of ship
wherefrom come the unknown unknowable voices
crying their who and their when and their where,
and then are withdrawn, as if they were silent,
or only to speak with the sound of the air:
and yet with a meaning, there seems to be meaning.

The light moves a trace to the right, and the heartbeat
shifts as in sympathy too with the light
the ear is now tuned to a new pitch of night
and begins all alone by itself to consider
something far off and absurd, a delight
but if so like a light with a cloud at its center,
and the cloud growing greater, the light growing less.

The fabric is bloodstream and bloodstream through measure
and measure through sense-ends and then shuttled back
for the heart and its courage to say yes to, or no to,
and the mind to twist into or out of a shape,
and the fancy, o fancy, what help from the fancy
that meddles and muddles and give itself airs
making riddles of loves and charades of despairs.

Step softly from here to the threshold of birth
the clock's tune and cock's crow and snare for the hare
the dew-betrayed footprint and the breath heard by fox
for death waits outside from the very beginning
our shadow precedes us and gives us our shape
and only in this shall we find out our dancing
and only in dancing find out our escape.

LOVE'S GRAMMARIANS

He
Periwinkle—bluet—Quaker Lady—
hear how the history of our love
echos in these nicknames
as now from the poetry book
we filch a phrase
to say all's over. The gods abandon
those who abandon the gods. There was no truth
in that fine vision we saw
under our Canaletto sunrise
nor at our sunset either
waiting by *traghetto* stairs
for the evening star's first footfall on water.
The fireflies are gone and the lanterns
from under the bridge. And we must run
for our very lives from those two fiends
so like ourselves
who even in the incredulous noon
would drag us back by the hair.
Once more permit them
and we are lost.

She

Presto—a melodrama—lost.
Do I guess what you mean by lost?
Is it an understatement? Do you mean
adulterated? But time and the rain
wash all away.

He

Lost in a repetitive nightmare
of our own invention. The deadly habit
obedient to the clock, and the clock
wound by an indifferent hand. Morning coffee
tiptoed to the bedroom, sherry among the orange trees,
dinner in the air-conditioned rock-garden.
And then the cigarette on the terrace
the whispering and withdrawing hour
while none keep guard at head of stair.
Time and place undid us.
Time's imperceptible sleight of hand
touching with curious frost
the simple heart. Use and satiety
dulling the sense until
nothing is left or only
an event which was over-prepared
for a body which was no longer concerned.
Love's grammarians were we ever?
But we no longer conjugate the tenses
or with each other
so let us part.

She

Time and place, time and place,
how dull you make them sound:
I'll take a happier ground.
A history and a mystery
of absurd but bewitching secrets
in the May sky tra la in the bloodstream too
in the gay heart and the merry mind
in the dream that sings on the borders of sleep
of worlds lost and worlds to come
all of it woven with needles of light
blossoming and vanishing
flashing and gone. Time and place
but with a difference. Everything
to be touched and loved at once
each fiery item intrinsic and tangible
as the round red moon of the calendar
or the seconds jumping like crickets
on the stupid face of the clock.
The senses are mischievous but also
there's magic in them, and love
lives through the senses only.
Isn't it there that the soul lies?
O yes and lies and lies if you like
for the soul too is a chameleon
where and for how long can it stand still?
Over the steeple and under the hill.
Yet volatile and incorporeal howsoever
—see where it flies!—
it too feeds only through the senses
summoning thus the very quiver of light
to be by this translated
and quickened to an ecstasy.
Now that is gone
and love undone.

He

So be it. For the last time I invoke
a particular moment. The clock strikes one.
A single snowflake floats against a pebble
clings to it with wings like a moth
and is gone. Our eyes
fill with a light till now unknown:
far recognitions, premonitions,
ethereal divinations
of all's that's past and to come.
Those histories and mysteries you speak of
the tangents of sense thrust against sense
but only the more to illumine:
the I and You become a phrase of music
obedient to a counterpoint
of earth air water and fire
which willy-nilly joins them.
Of this angelic confusion
what can we remember?
Only the snowflake falling.
While I for the first time
because it will be for the last time
observe with care the clear shape
of your closed eyelid.

She

Yes. Remember that. I too
have something to remember. I still see
under the umbrella's singing tent
how that rose-tinted shadow
changed a familiar face.
These shall be time and place.

THE ISLAND

Sly catbird it was you who first sang it
with your scrannel song
you among the small leaves
at the tip of the tree
singing it three times over
above the clover
        Do not go to that island
        no do not go to that far island
        it is morning, there is nothing to fear,
        stay here stay here.

Green spurge golden spurge you sang it again
from the top of the stone stair
in a wave of fragrance
sweeter than honey on the tongue of the bee
the wave of gold chiming it three times over
above the clover
        Do not go to that island
        never set sail for that inhospitable island
        there is nothing in the morning to fear
        stay here stay here.

Old heart it was you who then sang it
you with your ancient hourglass song
the song you brought with you from the sea
like a shell that sings of the sea in a green garden
whispering it three times over
above the clover
> Do not go to that unimaginable island
> never cast off to sail to that island
> morning is with us again
> stay here stay here.

two

The Tinsel Circuit

WILLIAMS & WILLIAMS

Curtains at last! The best of acts
goes stale. And then you dream
of dance and turn, and slide and turn,
until you'd like to scream.

Out there, a storm of violins,
while miles of footlights glare,
and we, we're only mannequins,
that step, and stop, and stare.

What fiend it is that pulls the strings,
and what it's for, god knows;
but we could strangle in the wings
whoever it is, that shows

no moment's mercy to the likes
of us who tread his measure,
and break our hearts, four times a day,
to give a moment's pleasure.

Come: we'll invent a change of scene:
the spotlight fizzing blue:
for a novelty called Hallowe'en,
with skulls for me and you.

SHARPE, MOSS AND LEWIS

Heavenly the scene was: how could she wait
for the magical moment when Moss made his exit—
'exiting right with a sneer and a gesture'—?
Rapture, sheer rapture! For now they could turn
and stare at each other, unashamed and unfeigning,
while slowly, so slowly, they moved to their meeting,
and at last touched hands!

Under her eyelids the footlights were swarming,
out in the dark was a murmur of faces,
but all she could see was the man she loved
(o and she did, for always and ever)
and all that he saw—he said—was a vision,
her hands lifted up in the light.
                The music, crescendo,
came like a full-moon tide underneath them,
sweet-sweet-sweet! cried Harry Frank's fiddles,
and the bull-frog double-bass throbbed. But then—
the whistle of terror came shrill at the door
and a bullet shattered the mirror behind them
and somebody screamed.

. . . Lovely, o lovely! Alone on the beach
she watched how the slow waves crested and crumbled,
and the seagull shadows flew over the foam,
and thought she never no never had loved him
never o never had ever loved anyone
as now she could love him in this silly scene.

EXIT

Yes, there he came, purple as an eggplant,
staggering out to the stage with a blue hand lifted,
and began reciting, for the fourth time that day,
The Face on the Bar-room Floor.
She stood in the wings to listen, but not with pity.
Watched the knees shaking, and the old adam's-apple,
and the fingernails white in the hard light. Noticed again
the red streaks under the ear, where fingernails
had scratched at eczema. The Face on the Bar-room Floor,
etched in sawdust, among cuspidors—old fraud,
he had come singing down the streets, all right,
while the gin lasted, and the voice lasted,
but now that adam's-apple would come to an end.
Brick—stone—dust—were all he had ever touched:
what valentines for him, who had no heart?
And now, and soon, over a windowsill,
in a dark room, on a bed by a speckled mirror,
the indifferent sun would find him dead.

Music must end, she thought, but after the ending,
when it is still, the wonder begins to be heard.
Why, why, it would seem to cry, why must we die?
The first-love rapture in moonlight,
who ever finds it again—? It is gone with its summer.
But to die like this, at the end of nothing,
in the wall-papered gloom of a furnished room,
to the sound of a cheap tin clock,
was it for this she hurried forever
down narrowing corridors to an unknown door?

45

THE TWO STERRETTS

You say men flirt with me, and you no longer like me,
because, you say, I let them. Maybe I do.
But if I do, whose fault is it, I wonder?
Right after we first teamed up,
who was it complained because I wasn't sexy?
You said I was tame, and put no life in the act,
that I was prudish and proper as a schoolgirl.
Well, I did as you told me. I put more life in the act,
and wore as little as a girl can get away with.
And what's the result? Surprise. They like it.
And now you complain because I'm not as proper
as the innocent kid you married.

I should have seen it coming. It's the old story—
pull a girl down to your own level, then kick her out,
sick of a thing too like yourselves. And then, why not,
comes somebody else—this doll in Vyo-Lyn!

No, chum, let's get this straight—I understand it.
You're tired of me, just as I'm tired of you.
I'm sorry, too, for at first I loved you—
I think I really did!
But there it is, and it might as well be faced.
Though, gosh, I almost wish we were starting over,
with the sense to see things right!

—She stirred her coffee,
and touched one eyelid to keep a tear from falling.
But he, absorbed in the smoke of a cigarette,
smiling a thin, self-conscious, ironic smile,
did not look up. Thinking that in two weeks
they'd come once more in the bill with Vyo-Lyn.

PROFESSOR LORRAINE

What worried him was, that he hadn't been drinking:
so how to explain it—? Those two middle fingers—
was that the trouble—were they getting stiff—?
He'd flipped the coins, and riffled the cards,
and flopped the rabbits out of the hat,
but then—the goldfish. Just as he started
to slip the bowl from the velvet cloth,
Christ!—And suddenly there they were
flapping all over the floor.

Eighteen years—count them, Professor.
The plain truth was, he was getting old.
Where had it gone? Marie was dead,
and the German girl, whose name he'd forgotten,
had flown the coop to be married.
And now, Felice, who stole his money,
laughed, when he dropped that goldfish bowl.

He put one hand out over the basin,
switched on the light with the other, stared
unhating unloving unknown unseeing
(but why he did it he couldn't have said)
at failure's face and a guilty hand
and turned on the taps and cried.

MARCH MIDNIGHT

Who cares where a man is buried, who cares, who cares?
Some like the country, some like the city,
there are trees in one and streets in the other,
but you don't get breakfast at seven in either,
and you don't get bills, and the mail is late.
As for my act, it wasn't too good, and it wasn't too bad,
but then, it was all that I had, and it's over.
                                    Just the same,
I'll admit that I had one fault—I was vain.
Vanity, vanity, said the preacher—
but not to me, for I wasn't there.
                                    Just the same,
do me a favor. Get out that suit
that I always wore, I wore it out—
purple, you know, with the eyes on the knees.
I'd like to see it again. I'd like to wear it
on my last ride to the not-so-golden gates.
Thanks. That's it. That's the one.

VIOLET AND LEOPARDS

Green eyes, and an emerald flicker behind them,
and when she cracked that blacksnake whip
you'd swear her eyes had done it.
Who was the watcher, who the watched?
Watching, whipping, prodding, cajoling,
cleaning up after them, trying to give them
the love they never accepted—
                              Out, now!—she'd cry—
Out, now! Out, now!—to snarl on pedestals
or leap through diamond hoops.
                              In, now! In, now!
Back to the cages! Live with animals,
become an animal. She was a leopard.

Sidelong she eyed you, sidelong she moved,
her eyes when they met you
gleamed and lost focus. Not strange
when the lights went down and the yellow cats
lapped round her in silence they seemed
as if summoned by magic out of herself
were only a dream and would vanish
back to the dark when the act was over.

Over. Not always. One night
one of the leopards went berserk. The spotlight man
shot down the light, where she stood,
safe as Brunnhilde in a circle of fire.
Now when she dreams she sees
her own heart torn, and hears bones cracking,
and eyes stare up unabashed from blood.

50

LISSOME LESTERS

Says Pierrot: You! Columbine!
Come down! The moon is hugely creeping,
and the stars begin to shine.

Says Pierrot: I'll take your hand
and guide you through the chattering dew
where ghosts flit over the sand.

Says Pierrot: I'll kiss your eyes
to such a sleep as that in which
the enchanted princess lies.

I'll play such a wicked melody
on the silver cobwebs of your hair
you'll give your heart to me.

Say no more, says Columbine:
I gave my paper rose to you,
and the stars begin to shine.

I gave my paper rose to you,
but if you seek my heart, who knows,
that may be paper too!

Two shadows dance, then pause to listen,
watching the music rise and glisten,
two shadows meet, and fade away,
hearing the moonlight play.

CURTAIN

When Vyo-Lyn have come and gone
and Queen Zudora's act is over
and Violet's leopard turn is done
and Felice runs to meet her lover

when cards and wands are laid away
and music stops and people hurry
and the dying man for one more day
postpones the fever and the worry

then, when the birds in hooded cage
are perched in silent rows and sleeping,
the redfaced stage-hand takes the stage,
and noisily goes across it, sweeping

the dust of golden-slippered feet,
spangles, and scraps of rainbow paper,
where Rose or Lily sang so sweet,
and Frost or Coffin cut a caper,

and having swept, turns out the lights,
and knocks his pipe, and leaves the curtain
hung high and dark for other nights,
and other vain things just as certain.

1916-1961

three

THE LOGOS IN FIFTH AVENUE

i

September, and Fifth Avenue, you said,
and said it somehow as if we both were dead:
and then as in an afterthought you said
'The first word on the tongue is it of love
and is our language, then, all love, each word
a kind of kindness, a kind of blessing?
                              The heart, therefore,
was named the heart because we love the heart?
Or was it that the heart became the word?'
It is absurd: we look for meaning, find
that we are lost in an algebraic surd.
The hurricane between us, or, in the morning press,
reports of changes in the style of dress,
the breastless female or the sexless male—
o god but how our history grows stale
if it is this we come to at the end
of god's beginning! Anguish, did you say?
Anguish unjust? God's anguish?
                              Play, play
the juke-box tunes of this unpopular day
the give-away and the say-hay-hay
forget the blind-man tapping with his cane
who will not see the autumn blue again
the newsboy with wet papers in the rain
the Big Board with its loss or gain:
excuse, or try to exorcise, the pain,
the anguish will remain.

As it should do,
as it should do. What would we be
if when the wind blows we
were not, and always, broken with the tree
the christ in us so broken?
                          What would we do
for fourth or fifth or heaventh avenue
and not with hope of recompense
or vanity of munificence
but with humility, and true?
Here is the locust tree, you see the thorns
it is the tree the tempest murdered, see
the starveling leaves stifled with soot
and suffer with the root
cramped under stinking asphalt!
                          Come away
for we have front row seats at the latest play,
The Lilies of Gomorrah, The Bells of Sodom,
and we will save our sorrows till tomorrow.

                    ii

Knock knock: knock knock: ring ring:
what will the morning postman bring?
Sufficient unto the day the bills thereof
no valentine no harbinger of love
no mockingbird upon the video tree
to promise us the spring
                          yet let him sing
above the neon lights in Ptomaine Row
sing for the library sing for the jail
yes and for all our lights that fail
as now they do. And we'll sing too
sing for the things we meant to do and be
the sunrise that we could not wake to see
the alms we did not give

            and the dear secret
found once, in the four-leafed clover, long since lost,
forgotten, or dissembled, or betrayed.

      iii

                  And now
take off the tarnished sock and go to bed
as if again we both were somehow dead
but as a prayer a remembered fraud of prayer
remember what you said.
                  What did I say?
Save it for another day.
                  What did I say?
Something of language, and of love, remember?
And something of September.
                  I did not say,
I merely asked. Asking is all we seem
as in a waking dream
to be able or partly able
to do. We wait for knockings on a table
                  which when they come
are random false or meaningless or dull.
                  Better to knock on wood
as someone said!
                  And did he mean a tree?
Better to go to bed and *scream*
when nightmare rears its eyeless head
from the mythic waters of sleep.
                  Better to keep
even in sleep as now you do
the something that you said you thought was true
the something borrowed with something *blue*.
                  And yes,
blue was for the blind-man, blue was for the sky,
blue was for the eye—
                  I am not I.

      57

iv

Morning empties the garbage pails of night
morning empties the sky of clouds the mind of dreams
and see, the dapple-grey coursers of the sun
beat up the dawn with their bright silver hooves.
It was not I who said this, was not you,
and yet we know it true.
                              For the dream kept,
as the dream always does, while still you slept,
under the quilt and under the guilt
and the starless waters of sleep,
what we could not endure and not forget
the perdurable time
which, as the telltale dream admits,
is of the nature of a crime.
                              Listen:
a bell unthinking in unthinking sky
mocks the resentful ear, as at the eye
teases the minatory light of morning.
                              Wake!
and face reality once more, reality
which in its finite wisdom permits us each to die
but will not die itself!
                              Return
out of the flight of dream to face
the fever and the fret, the sad St. Vitus
dance of the hours, the god's and ours,
amid the drear detritus
that blows along the one-way street
                              while at the corner
waits by the silver-wreathèd Cadillac
the undertaker's shiny black
                              sole mourner
for someone's Little Boy Blue or lost Jack Horner
and the meek body that was his share of god.

Today
we will again be circumspect
we know what to expect
the iceman with his fifty pounds of ice
nuns in a flutter at the convent door
                    the scattered rice
left for the pigeons from the wedding-day
and fifty sample bedrooms to inspect.
And in those fifty bedrooms who will sleep
as we this night or keep
vigil even in dream?
                    The tugboats mourn
in immemorial weather, the southeast wind
brings from the harbor rain, the clang
of ashcans rings on asphalt
                    but our dream our dream
with a timepiece precision seems to keep
its tiny tick of truth.
                    Take out your chalk
and on sidewalk as for hopscotch mark
the humble squares for devious progress: not
as in our childhood blossom root or leaf
nor rich man poor man beggarman thief
but drugstore movie bar and car
garage post office hospital morgue
subway and comfort station. Shall we play?
in this poor hierarchy find our way?
Listen to what they say: 'Gee mom my tongue is dirty.'
'How can it be? It's in your mouth.'
                    Or, 'Don't be stupid, kid,
dogs can't chew gum.'
                    Better to pray
remembering what you said.
                    What did I say?
And that was yesterday!

                                    Better today
to take a taxi up Fifth Avenue
visit the sealions at the Zoo
stop for a beer at the Shamrock Bar and see
a baseball game or prizefight on TV.

                    V

The siren wails, but not from the far islands,
nor for divine Ulysses, but down the street
to fire or death. The bent cat in the alley
slinks his despair. Under the tree of heaven
cheep-cheep cheep-cheep the dusty sparrows
forage for gravel.
                            On his stoop the priest
blank-faced now takes the air
an interval of blankness between prayer
intonements for atonement without meaning.
But you too something said of prayer.
                        I did not say of prayer
but as a remembered fraud of prayer
ritual of beseeching from childhood's teaching.
Yet it was true if as a reaching
of mind and hand to understand beyond
what we were taught as true and, yes, still true.
                        And is still true, for you?
Still true, but in a different way.
                            What did you say?
What was it that you said and took to bed
so that we dreamed it both and loved it both
yes loved it knee to knee the I becoming we?

                    I said
each face of all we meet will soon be dead
I said the child is father to the corpse
I said the skeleton is in the womb
I said the city is a honeycomb
a honeycomb of tomb and there we move
or think we move who are already still
and there we love or think we love
                    and yet
perhaps we should not emphasize alone
the brevity of life the levity of stone.
Though this cathedral mausoleum fall
                    as fall it must and come to dust
and with its splendors us
                    still let us not forget
the nowness of the hand upon the bough,
the nowness of the now.
The living moment of the dream
with its timepiece precision watching truth
still keeps eternal youth
not only in the solar month and year
but always, and forever, here.
                    Stay, stay,
the hand upon the bough upon the heart
stand still o love o living art
that in the blood and in the sap and in the sun
as in our mythic dream last night
bids all remain unchanged:
urge now your love for all things demiurge
for that is he and that is we
and bid this pattern be.

A IS FOR ALPHA: ALPHA IS FOR A

i

Now it begins. Now the subaqueous evening
exemplary as the inalterable moon
begins again to begin. With slight starts
of organ-grinder music (if the scene
is of city) or of—'dee-dee-dee—!'
chickadee trill if (as it is) it is country.
The shadow, complex, seven-branched, of the ancient lyre-tree
prolongs itself on the sensual lawn and fades away
predicting a reverse shadow at daybreak. The star
(for look, love, there is a star)
trills through the sunset like a bird
diamond point in crimson word
and melts, and we are heard.
So, now, the casual evening begins, and its slow texture
weaves us into a casuistry. We, who were just now thoughtless,
or lost in a loss of thought,
come to a breaking and dissolving
sunset of our own. The world ends
and another begins. The love ends
—or does it?—
and another begins. But the light
lasts forever, there is no night.

The hands you lift are sunset, and the hands
are the exemplary moon. The eyes you lift
change with the texture of the evening,
Venus it might be one way, Sirius the other;
the lengthening shadow, so intricate, so various, of the lyre-tree
prolongs our listening nerves into the coming light
of tomorrow. My love, observe a moon
unobserved by any till now. Bland and bleak
as any lovestruck human. Such as we?
Such as we. We are the silver rind
of moonlight, for now it hardens, now is crystal,
on this tree, this virgin locust tree, and we
are moon and tree.

Fade, fade, all into darkness fade,
but also into light
since one the other closes.
The texture of the evening is of roses,
and we are, for the moment, roses too.
Love is not much: it is a touch: but it is true.

      ii

Evening, which evens all things. Hand in hand
brindled by sunset thought we stand
prolonging our nerves, and with them nature, into another day.
We are the sacred players and the play:
we are the music, and what the musicians say:
and always our new title is Today.
Today, and yesterday; the divine dance
moves under heart and heaven, the wave of light
gathers its all for a breaking of time
and then falls inward. We are the rhyme
paired like two words in love, and move
in the twinned discord of a chord, our love
hidden in its own secret, like the rose.
Will the rose unclose, disclose?
finding—how naturally!—a reason for season?

63

It is ourselves that open, even
to the innermost heaven.
It is ourselves magically disguised
as harp-string and harp-song, birdsong and petal,
ice-metal, rain-metal,
ourselves curving the air with a wing
ourselves the air for the wing to find and follow
ourselves the sunlight and the swallow.
Divisibly indivisible we sing
the begin-all-end-all thing:
night becomes a god, and we the night,
for the unfolding and enfolding of our delight.

       iii

Intervals and interstices of texture
enthrall us, bring us to a standstill, bemuse
fingertip and eyebeam, idea and eye;
while the mind fills with wonders. The voice
is of what? Who said to it, 'rejoice'?
You there, I here; you with your mountains of snow,
and your seven golden seas, and the woven Nile,
and the sky piled high with purple clouds;
and I with my rocky Sahara, ribbed with lapis lazuli,
and the last sail melting into sunset:
these are the language of interval, the interstices
subtle and gigantic, unfathomable, inaudible,
hieroglyphic and hieratic, by which we speak.
The exchange is golden. It is thesaurus. The exchange
beggars us only then to endow us again,
exhausts us only to replenish. The simple rain
walking before us down the country lane
shuttling before us down the country lane
says it with silver, syllables it slowly,
repeats its holy, holy,
and into it, and into night,
we weave this love, this light.

THE RETURN

Dear tiger lily, fanged and striped! you are the bravest,
you as well as another will serve to chant
tongued with flame our vernal madrigal,
sowing among sequins of last year's locust
love's golden rhetoric:
you and the celandine
of immaculate green.
Wraiths of snow run from the stallion sun,
quicksilver lizards of water
flick their tails into cisterns,
and on the tarnished grass
where north wind sheered his drifts
in phantom edifice
melts the last sickle of pale ice:
and there, in a little while, where late was snow
the Indian Pipes will blow.
O darling, listen—from the orchised bog
chuckles the ancient and omniscient frog
his gross venereal hymn:
and the reed-scented wind, the bulrush-rattling wind,
dreams like memory through the mind.
Now love returns once more, our lost and antique love,
dear tiger lily! above
the sad detritus of death:

65

fling we then out of doors and into hearts,
where the year freshly starts,
and join the song-sparrow
in Hymen's favorite song:
for treason late and long,
yes, the sly shibboleth
of treason to death, and love, and another season!

The oak leaves rustle in the thicket,
loosen themselves, detach, and fall,
pale brown, pale purple, harsh still;
the hawk hangs over his beloved hill
as love hangs over the destined heart:
and once more joyfully we begin
the ancient dance of meet and part,
                              wherein
each is in turn the hawk and each the heart.
We touch and meet, we touch and greet,
kiss gravely, tread apart,
next glance, and eye askance,
curtsey in courtship's bashful dance,
retreat, and then advance.
O unknown love
unknown and treacherous as that sky above
and as my own heart is,
what is the meaning of your kiss?
Each lover asks and answers this
in blinded bliss.
Glad, glad, the sound
of two hearts beating, together bound,
O but tumultuous the rest
of your face, love, that rests upon my breast,
tumultuous the rest
of each upon the other resting:
two worlds at war we are,
star dancing against star.

For each must learn in each
all the dark-rooted language under speech:
here, look! new love, the roots we did not know,
strong stems, deep stains, rich glories never guessed:
disparate origins and desperate sins,
acknowledged or unacknowledged, understood
or misunderstood; the labyrinthine windings
through the lewd galleries of the mind, to find
something or nothing; illusory findings
which vanish at the touch, or on exposure to the air,
and of which, only in default, are we aware;
hatred derived from love, love from terror,
the roots not knowing their own fruits;
the unpracticed, and then the all-too-practiced vices,
deliberate dishonesties and rehearsed voices;
purpose becoming mean, meanness purpose,
wants promoted to obsessions, and the obsessions
near to madness. Who am I, who are you,
that one to the other must be true, untrue,
or dissect untrue from true?
Who shall possess, or be possessed? possession
of how much? of what ecstasy, or for what duration?
Where, too, and in what characters shall we meet
playing what parts of the multitude we have played
wearing what masks and shabby costumes
on the strewn stage of habit? The attitudes
are predictable, and therefor false, they belong
to another situation, are the inheritance
of other loves and lusts. What beatitudes
can the wingèd god invoke from these? In what divine dance
instruct these stained and stinking puppets?
Out of such mouths what song, what song?

And yet the tiger lily, under the snow,
heedless alike of year ago or long ago,
and the endless history of her repeated love,
dares yet again to thrust above
the sad detritus of death, and grow:

and speaks with the song-sparrow the sly shibboleth
of another season, another treason!
Lost memory, lost love, lost to return,
can we, too, not be brave like these, relearn
O as if all were virginal and new
the hawk and heart of 'I' and 'You'?
O daring darling, can we not trust
once more that innocent sky
once more to break our hearts and die?

Comes now, comes she!
comes the unknown, the unpredictable,
she who is half spring, half summer,
between the lilac and the wrinkled apple blossom,
the unknown, all-unimagined newcomer,
birch foot, beech heart, myrtle hand,
and the indecipherable mind
and virgin bosom
and windflower grace
and timeless Etruscan pace
and the tiger's heart, cruel to be kind:
comes like the sunshot southwest wind
bidding the elm bough, soliciting
the fan of iris under the snow
for one more spring, one more spring:
while the hawk's wing
sickles the white-blossoming hill
with shadow of death, the scythe's shadow
shadowing the redwing into the meadow.
O innocence in guilt, and guilt in innocence,
she stoops, she hovers,
fiercest and subtlest, and yes, tenderest of lovers,
the ruthless one
whose eye is in the sun.

THE WALK IN THE GARDEN

i

Noting in slow sequence by waterclock of rain
or dandelion clock of sun
the green hours of trees and white hours of flowers:
annotating again the 'flower-glory of the season,
a book that is never done,' never done:
savoring phrases of green-white, mock-white,
while the ancient lyre-tree, the ancient plum,
adds for another May its solar sum
in silent galaxies of bloom:
it is here, interpreting these, translating these,
stopping in the morning to study these,
touching affectionately the cold bark
of the seven-branched tree, where bees
stir the stars and scatter them down:
it is here, in these whitenesses of thought,
poring over these pages of white thought,
that we ponder anew the lifelong miracle:
the miracle that in these we best remember,
and in wisdom treasure best,
the lost snows of another December,
and the lost heart, and the lost love.
What matter that we are older, that we age?
Blest that we live this morning, blest
that still we read the immortal book
and in time's sunlight turn another page.

69

ii

Shall we call it, then, the walk in the garden?
the morning walk in the simple garden? But only if by this we mean
everything! The vast daybreak ascends the stairs of pale silver
above a murmur of acacias, the white crowns
shake dark and bright against that swift escalation of light,
and then, in intricate succession, the unfolding minutes and hours
are marked off by the slow and secret transactions
of ant and grassblade, mole and tree-root,
the shivering cascade of the cicada's downward cry, the visitation
(when the brazen noon invites) of that lightninged prism
the hummingbird, or the motionless hawkmoth.
Listen! The waterclock of sap in bough and bole,
in bud and twig, even in the dying
branch of the ancient plum-tree, this you hear, and clearly,
at eleven, or three, as the rusted rose-petal
drops softly, being bidden to do so, at the foot of the stem,
past the toad's unwinking eye! Call it
the voyage in the garden, too, for so it is:
the long voyage home, past cape and headland
of the forgotten or remembered: the mystic signal
is barely guessed in the spiderwort's golden eye, recognized
tardily, obscurely, in the quick bronze flash
from the little raindrop left to wither
in the hollow of a dead leaf, or a green fork
of celandine. For in this walk, this voyage,
it is yourself, the profound history of your 'self,'
that now as always you encounter. At eleven or three
it was past these folded capes and headlands, these decisions or refusals,
these little loves, or great,
that you once came. Did you love? did you hate?
did you murder, or refrain from murder, on an afternoon
of innocent cirrus in April? It is all recorded
(and with it man's history also)
in the garden syllables of dust and dew:

70

the crucifixions and betrayals,
the lying affirmations and conniving denials,
the cowardly assumptions, when you dared not face yourself,
the little deaths, and the great. Today
among these voluntary resumptions you walk a little way
toward tomorrow. What, then, will you choose to love or hate?
These leaves, these ants, these dews, these steadfast trifles, dictate
whether that further walk be little or great.
These waiting histories will have their say.

iii

But of those other trifles, the too intrusive,
the factual, the actual, that are too intrusive,
too near, too close, too gross, for deeper meaning:
what of these, what will memory make of these?
Will these too yield in time to the magic of translation?
The bobby-pins, the daily news, the paper-clips, even
the stuffed two-headed calf once seen in a pawnshop window;
as indeed also the crumpled letter, furtively
dropped in the ashcan at the corner,
yes, and the torn half of the movie ticket, bright pink,
found inadvertently in the breast-pocket, to remind you—
but meanly—of other days of afternoon rain:
how will you profitably rehearse these,
how will you (otherwise than here!) rehearse these,
        and to what end
of reconstruction? for what inspired reinterpretation
of the lost image, the lost touch?
Useless, here, the immediate, the factual, the actual:
the telephone remains silent when most you wish to hear it:
the May morning, or is it August or September,
remains empty, infertile, at precisely that instant
when your heart—if that is what you mean by heart—
would invoke a vision.

Blessing enough, indeed, it might have been,
but not under peach-tree or lyre-tree,
in the persistence of the radio's tremolo
and the listening silence of an empty room:
blessing enough if in these should quietly have spoken,
in answer to that invocation, the not-voice of voice,
the now almost unknown and unfamiliar voice,
the voice at first not recognized when heard:
blessing enough if in these
indifferent accidents and meaningless impromptus
the angelic not-you should open the door
and angelically enter, to take slow possession
of the room, the chairs, the walls, the windows,
the open piano with its waiting keys,
and the poor bed under the forgotten picture,
but possessing also
the divine touch that in the radiant fingertips
could at once create, with a magician's eloquence,
nothing from something, or something from nothing:
as, out of the untouched piano,
a shabby chord, a threadbare tune, the banal air
squealing from the midnight juke-box, where,
at the corner saloon, over the tepid beer,
you sit and stare,
remembering how the days have become years,
and the minutes hours,
and the false sunlight is distilled to tears
in the sentimental involutions of a shared sound:
yes, and the touch of the fingertip, once, on the back of the hand,
or, for a braver instant, tentatively, along the line of the cheek:
but no, these are all a broken imagination only,
the one and only heart remains lonely,
the morning remains silent, cannot speak,
muted by the ridiculous trifles, the preposterous trifles,
that stammer between the past and you.

Only, in the thinking hands, for a moment,
the persistent stupid bloodstream vaguely traces—
as if on air, as if on air—
the lost touch, the lost image, the chimerical future:
praying, now, for the illusion of an abstract love.

iv

The illusion of an abstract love? Say, rather,
it was the loves and hates that were illusion,
and all that accompanied them: items of fatigue
or of dubious regret, denials and acceptances,
these it is that are as clouds
gone deathward over the morning, lost, dislimned,
and now recoverable only, if at all,
in the remembered crevice in the remembered garden wall:
abstracted out of space, abstracted out of time,
but now reset, by the morning walk in the garden,
in crystal rhyme.
In these rich leaves, which are not only leaves
of lyre-tree or pomecitron, but also leaves
of a living book that is never done:
from winter to summer, from spring to fall:
in these we keep them all.
Here is that abstract love which we would find
wherein all things become imperishable mind:
the numberless becomes one, the brief becomes everlasting,
the everlasting opens to close
in the perishing of the raindrop on the rose:
violence is understood, and at last still,
evil is fixed and quiet as a tree or hill,
but all alike acceptable and one
and in one pattern made to move, or not to move,
by the illusion, if it is illusion,
of an abstract love.

Touch now again the serpent skin of the lyre-tree:
stoop now again, a hummingbird,
to the magic of the mock-orange:
count again by waterclock of rain
or dandelion clock of sun
the slow days of trees, the quick hours of flowers:
this time, this matin-song, this love, is yours, is ours,
a book that is never done, never done.

OVERTURE TO TODAY

This day is not as other days: will not be
a pale and stencilled pattern of those others:
the golden nexus of the dream
from which you woke at six in a thrill of rain
the golden wall from which an unknown woman leaned and spoke
calling your name, and then
put forth her hand to touch your face
saying, 'This day
will not be as those others, come, we will go away
into another world, another city, where
each avenue will be light, each house a prayer
and song the equivalent of breath!'
       Fair, fair,
shines in the dream the dream's unfolding
from be to seem
from chaos into shape
from fear from death
yet with at first what slow and leaden step
we strive towards the wings of our escape
into that other country, where,
caught in a rarer pattern of intent,
we draw an exquisite and conscious breath!
       Design,
as in the intricate dream, in us is woven:
and like the multiple meaning of the dream
which changes as it gleams, we too
are ravelled out in fiery threads:

under the very mind's-eye reappear
the thousand faces and the thousand eyes,
in every facet of the hour,
with which ourselves ourselves surprise.
                              Seed to flower:
and flower to seed. The hourglass turns
and pours its golden grains. The animal lives
mysteriously to himself, ordained, inviolable,
in a compulsive dream. The human child
so lives too without knowing,
innocent, living at one with the earth, the mother,
innocent participant of death and birth
and of begetting. Yet he must wake
and in the moment of his waking take
terrible knowledge of the miracle that is self.
See how he stands enringed
by the angelic and demonic powers, the winged
and fanged and finned and clawed!
And awed, and overawed,
now fades his song of innocence
                              and now begins
anthem of earth and heaven,
a new and richer counterpoint of praise,
that with experience is given:
henceforward he can sing
a fairer thing:
the radiant mysteries
that now are shared, and his.
                              Profound, profound,
celestial, or underground, or truly found
even in the hand's sore breadth, and the eye's beam,
as in the golden nexus of the dream,
the god of order like a golden worm
working in all things to his perfect term:
the golden rivet, reason, manifest
but only to our simple eyes in simplest form:
the mysteries
mostly impenetrable except in these, as these:

the pure simplicity of the flower
the little flower for the first time seen
above her shadow in her transparency of hour:
time taking transient shape in this, as time
takes shape in us who see
and in the foreforged word and chthonic rhyme
with which we bid it pause and be.
Who would not worship at the heart, the tree?
                              And we
who are the source of all delight and light
in which the meaning of the song stands still
are part and parcel of the mystery.

             ii

And so, this day is not as others: no day
repeats the others. Yet what it brings
out of the instant past in its succession
for you the palimpsest of a dream, for the wild rose
time to open or to close,
time for the dead leaf to be crystal in the brook
for the opening or the shutting of the book
time for the oak to add another druid ring,
time to explore, time to explain
precisely why at six o'clock in a throb of rain
the cry of the pure heart was caught in a dream
precisely why
in the child's round vowel of song, or in the bird's
sleepy roulade, or in a myth, or a rune of words,
or on the blackboard in the school
where calligraphic chalk unfolds
a geometric golden rule;
design and the designer are the same,
the namer is the name.
                              We who divine,
waking or sleeping, or in the manifold dream,
define, then redefine,

by rule of thumb or harmony of number
seeking tomorrow's validity in curve or line or cosine
and in the eye that measures or in the thought
that through its own closed finite world of sense
        takes measured flight
and always starting over, every day
brought to a standstill by the same or a different doubt,
the imagination like a kite reeled in
and then again reeled out:
       we who divine
divine ourselves, divine our own divinity
        it is the examination
of godhead by godhead
        the imagination
of that which it is to be divine.

   iii

Six o'clock. The tiger dream relinquishes
the traumatic heart. The tiger rain
claws at the windowpane
       and before we sleep again
the bell strikes in the remembering heart
and as in a lightning-flash of time
      we see
backward into the abyss of all we know and are.
Wings in the night fly left and right
swarm downward and away, and far,
only the cry of sky
       floats upward, 'What am I?'
Yes, what am I? from what arriving? and into what
ascending or descending? The multiple dream
assembles its mythic fragments, like a kaleidoscope
clicks them into a pattern. We begin
to know, or think we know, to understand
or think we understand. Then sleep again.

iv

Before the unknown day which is to come
from east and past and earth and sky
arriving like the tumid tide that swells
under the precursive and magnetic moon
and bringing like the tide its ancient freight
of solar and human history, we wait
veiled in a hushed anticipation, conscious of the hour
and yet unconscious also since its power
not in the marker of the bell but in the swell
of tidal mystery without within
is ours as well as time's. In a pure state
of irresponsible expectancy, of pregnancy,
like those who wait to see
a theatre's curtain drawn and what is there to be,
we wait, and stare, and know
that this will be no ordinary show:
that something godlike here begins
                                and greater far
than our poor dream may have conception of:
                                and yet
it is ourselves who have conceived
and have believed
that what we see will be the work of love.
                                This day
will be the enacting of that foredoomed play.

And now the musicians of the heart begin
with heartbeat drum and flute of truth
and tender violin, begin
the sacred overture:
                                at first the pure
song of the child the song of innocence
and daybreak air

                  and then the sober prayer
and anthem of experience
                mature and sure
with contrapuntal weavings in and out
of love and wonder, faith and doubt,
             and last
the many-voiced hymn of wisdom,
                in which the past
of innocence and experience become one
the end implicit in the beginning
                    but all one . . .
                  And now the sun
divides the curtains of the night; our play,
of which the title is Today, will be begun.

What will it be? We do not know. But it will say:
love is the action which brings forth the day,
whether of will to love or will to live:
the necromancer's genius which brings forth
the golden All from the golden Nothing.
Love is poetry, the god's recreation,
his joy in *fiat,* the world becoming word.
It is creation and recreation, two words in one,
the poem always just begun
and never done.
                The world as word
this is the poem which the wise poet writes
in us and through us and around us writes
                o and invites
all things created, and all things to come,
each to make tribute and contribution make
to what is never whole
                or wholly heard.

four

THE WINDOW

She looks out in the blue morning
and sees a whole wonderful world
she looks out in the morning
and sees a whole world

she leans out of the window
and this is what she sees
a wet rose singing to the sun
with a chorus of red bees

she leans out of the window
and laughs for the window is high
she is in it like a bird on a perch
and they scoop the blue sky

she and the window scooping
the morning as if it were air
scooping a green wave of leaves
above a stone stair

and an urn hung with leaden garlands
and girls holding hands in a ring
and raindrops on an iron railing
shining like a harp string

an old man draws with his ferrule
in wet sand a map of Spain
the marble soldier on his pedestal
draws a stiff diagram of pain

but the walls around her tremble
with the speed of the earth the floor
curves to the terrestrial centre
and behind her the door

opens darkly down to the beginning
far down to the first simple cry
and the animal waking in water
and the opening of the eye

she looks out in the blue morning
and sees a whole wonderful world
she looks out in the morning
and sees a whole world.

VOYAGE TO SPRING

Dry the grass this September, dry the whistle
of the quail searching the cranberry bog for water,
and the cicada's little helicopter
spins sadly down in sunlight, like a child's toy
running down at once in tone and time.
To be immersed now in a vision of rank spring again,
with all its powers and vicissitudes, its falseness too,
yet with its powers commensurate to its dream,
how inopportune, but with what persuasive logic
the notion shuttles (in, at last, the late afternoon rain)
through the warped summer! *We could have lived, we could live*—
so in susurrus whisper the perished grassblades
and the shrivelled plums that drop from the ancient plum-tree:
we could have loved, we could love—
rhythmic as the complaint of the crickets on a night of frost.
And the slow rain, the gentle resurrection of rain,
leaf-bobbing rain, twig-dripping rain,
walks down the road as if it were a vein
from which such visions might yet come again.

As so, indeed, they do. The natural magic
of natural things: the rain evokes the rain,
and that another. How the long quaver rises
in ghostly shimmer of fruitful deception.
Out of this, things came to pass—out of this,
the dream, the reality, the vision, and the fact.

I am what I was, I was what I am, I would like to be
what I am no longer. For the poor benefit
of a lost moment of sensual satisfaction,
the nymph-cry in the blood, the whimpered rainsong
of the beloved under one's kiss, the all-night-rainsong,
the *I-can-love, I-can-love,*
how one would sacrifice one's integrity, pretend
to be what one no longer is, envying those
who need no pretence, who in their natural spring
invent an April! Useless to remind the lovers
while still they are locked in undivided delight
in their self-woven chrysalis of night
that this is not an end or a beginning
nor a single birth nor a single death nor climax
nor an exploration nor a discovery nor a voyage
but the gross usufruct, indifferent and mechanical,
automatic as the bursting of a seed-pod,
of life itself, the source and sink of all.
Useless, too, to tell oneself. One looks and envies,
one listens and envies, longing only again to know
the accelerated heart-beat, the blind passion to touch,
the inexhaustible need for surrender, the suffocation
of anguish that one feels in separation,
and the unappeasable suffocation of desire
of each to be incorporated in the other.
False, false, false, all of it false,
the necessary inevitable illusion, chromatic deception
of the vernal and venereal equinox: the mere rubescence
of old whore earth in the spring.

ii

                     For the chromatic deception,
the viridescent treason, is everywhere: the blush
is merely the signal of deceit. How all nature
is riddled with design, yes, raddled with it too,
old harridan that she is. How with low cunning
she baits her trap with a young anxious body,
and that with agate eyes, and those with a radiance
beautiful and bent as sunlight through sea-foam:
and the small mouth, *bocca tremante,* trembling and timid,
that asks but says no, denies but says yes—
with what pathos, what tremulous empathy,
prefiguring all, foretasting all,
it offers to be shaped, or to shape itself, to yours—
which could have shaped itself to many, and in time
will find the time to do. For did you think
to have fidelity in nature? No such thing.
She is a broker, she must make money breed.
All her investments are short-term loans, callable
at notice. Let the young anxious body, the *bocca tremante,*
and the desired smile, *disiato riso,* fail in their purpose,
it is only for a moment, they will be tried again.

And with the necessary attributes, the requisite
décor, the illusory stage effects, all supplied
—as in a theatre programme—by yourself:
which is to say by Eros, the imagination.
Such sunsets, too. Sunsets to beggar description
and dissolve the reason, each with a chemical
affinity for the blood, and wired for sound
to the very psyche: while the off-stage aria
eerily haunts the wings with an evocation
of deus-ex-machina, the oracular, the all-too-divine.

87

Everything becomes of a texture exquisitely suited
to the lover's touch: preposterously precious:
the rock-surfaces are of silk, screened through desire,
and even the vulgarest landscape, mere terrestrial segment,
the broken billboard in a vacant lot,
is translated in a twinkling to translunar.

And then the music: the by-no-means
so incidental music—O god that music.
For what's in music that it so probes a lover's pain,
nesting even in the embolism? The threadbare scrape of catgut
tangles the gullible and hallucinated heart
with the music of the spheres, no less.

And what's to be treasured of this, what's kept
of the off-stage aria, the pinchbeck golden sunset
on a more than Roman scene? What's left of these
fine shades, and shades of shades, those O so delicate
distinctions and divinations, those rare tremors
projected by the lover's eye, his heart, his mind?
Nothing, or less than nothing: since it is something
chimerical as the blood-count in a raindrop:
and the wide arch of the deranged empire falls.
No, not in love comes summer from spring, no, never.
Nor is its dream, the dear dream (and we thought
its powers commensurate to its dream)
ever fulfilled. Not what the lover willed,
but something else, is kept: and while he slept.

iii

Yes, in the rain, in the autumn, in the memory,
the silence that follows the cicada's silence,
the footsteps of the rain gone down the lane
seeking a vision that will not come again
(or will it, do we find it now)
but most of all in memory, mine and yours,
the sad by-product of the sad by-product mind,
and most, most of all in the sad by-product mind—
O traitor love, perhaps in this we keep
something that will not fail us, even in sleep:

Perhaps in the notation of the deception,
the riddling out of the illusory colours
with which old nature baits her trap, in the loving
and agonized appraisal of the young anxious body,
and the agate eyes, and the small mouth, *bocca tremante,*
that asks to shape itself to yours:
and in the knowing, and the pain of knowing, also,
the response, the answer, automatic in onself:
yes, in this miserable knowledge, that destroys, as it learns,
heart-beat by heart-beat the passion it feeds on,
is our escape, our one escape. The mirage of spring
shatters about us in a broken prism of rainbows
never to be assembled again, or to be assembled
only in the ironic despair of a dream:
the false sunset has vanished under more than the sea:
the stage is suddenly vaster, there are no wings
for the off-stage voice of the pseudo-god:
instead, the silence and loneliness of self
become a new world, of which the shores
are faintly audible, faintly visible. We will go there.

MORITURA

Three o'clock, and the surf of wind in the locusts
pours the quick moonlight through pooled or cascaded leaves:
O destructive and creative agony of the living leaves
at three o'clock in the morning of death in life.

For she has no heart, and I have no heart,
as we lie and listen to the agony of dying leaves:
it is our own rich agony we hear in the dying leaves
at three o'clock in the morning of death in life.

'There is ever,' she murmurs, 'a shadow of *moritura*
in anything really beautiful': and our love lies bleeding,
even in the first kiss our love lies bleeding,
at three o'clock in the morning of death in life.

Can we bid the image stay? or hold it trembling
in love's Narcissus pool for one shared moment?
O destructive and creative agony of the changing moment
at three o'clock in the morning of death in life.

The song-sparrow's song is fixed on the dawn like a pattern of silver
rises and falls in the dark like a pattern of silver
and the death of our love is fixed in a pattern of silver
at three o'clock in the morning of death in life.

Yes, in this deep embrace, we lie divided:
'For the death of all experience,' she murmurs again,
'is the shadow beside the experience, runs beside it,'
at three o'clock in the morning of death in life.

There, down the stairs of the blood, we hear it hurry,
light-footed ghost of change, the beautiful death,
and already our love is the moss torn away from the rockface
at three o'clock in the morning of death in life.

'Rest here, rest nowhere,' so says the surf in the trees.
'Rest here, rest nowhere,' says the heartless woman beside me.
For she has no heart, and I have no heart,
at three o'clock in the morning of death in love.

THE IMPROVISATION

The synthesis of spring once more, antique illusion:
the icicle slips from the eaves and is brilliantly shattered,
the dog-tooth violet pricks her ears under leaf-mould:
but not in April, and later than Indian Summer.
The bird, that we heard in our orchard,
let him remain unknown and nameless,
the fabulous harbinger of a chimerical season.
And who would have thought the hylas would wake November,
chant their plain-song in November?
Now systole and diastole should be hushed
mortally under snow, slowed to the rhythm
of water under ice on a night of planets.
Instead, comes the ragged celandine
brashly out of orbit, and the song-sparrow's rehearsed roulade
charms the breathless caesura of sunrise
wholesome and formal as a passage of Haydn.
Solecism of solstices: winter the dupe of spring:
or together the two in a dialectic
ghostly as moonlight at midday.

And the rituals, the formalities, the prepared language,
how inadequate to the occasion: for none exist.
The bloodroot unfolding under ice? the little Lady's Slipper
under snow? while the poor blue-bird,
lost between weathers, his time-sense confused as ours,
startles with colour the cavernous iceberg.

We were not born, surely,
to be thus confronted. The Great Astrologer's eyepiece
slipped from his eye for a moment, and the two particles
escaped all knowledge. And so, out of time,
and only of our own volition,
together drawn by an outlaw motion,
we reach the intangible, touch the inaccessible,
by our own privilege know the Unknown.

Yes, and with what precarious, hesitant, yet archangelic improvisation,
everything foreseeing, we make the slow footsteps
of love into music: as easily and naturally
as the sly catbird, luckiest of singers, builds his madrigal
into the nuptial nest. The approach, the half-meeting,
the hands eager to touch, almost touching, yet not touching,
the stillness, and the pause, the weighing of the laws
that move the measured footsteps towards obliteration,
and then at last, as if in air, sudden as a wing-beat,
the meeting itself—
                                        whether through the eyes,
which can never have enough of light,
or through the hands, which can never have enough of touch,
or the voices, which, for joyful humility,
fall incredulous into silence—

these we compose intricately, with radiant certainty,
point counterpoint, the luminous algebra of love,
(it is as if our veins became skeins of light)
into our passacaglia, which now trembles
by right successions to its ecstasy.

And so the ending: for inevitably it ends.
Brightness falls from the air, and the moving dance
of the unseen dancers, who danced on light,
is over, and with it our shining.

The music is ended: yet after it falls
the wave of silence on which the music was written,
the moment of the music's wholeness, when we hear
the All in the single instant of time. Love ends
where it begins: the birth and the renunciation
are one, one and the same.

Fair indeed was the deceitful summer: halcyon the afterglow
in which we loose our thistledown towards winter:
August's fireflies are hurried to a phantom death
far from the rose-garden, by the metal rocks of Labrador:
and we die with them, they are ourselves.

ii

And of the bodies: the minds: the memories,
thus capriciously brought together: we who have neither
acquired nor inherited formulae for living, who love
from one soul's-instant to another, as we live:
always the giant step from island to island of being
terrified yet fearless over the infinite,
precisely as the celandine steps from November
to blind April, the season of death to the season of procreation:
what will they make of this unstellar conjunction?
propose what cavils and confusions? with what protocol
solemnize the meeting of self and not-self?
Hardened travellers, each with his own luggage
of habit and injury!

Let us not be afraid, for all is acceptable,
unknown past and unknown future alike acceptable:
the stepping-stones of the known to the past,
and the stepping-stones of the known to the future,
will lead us, item by sunlit item, till we drown in light.

Dear stranger, in whom the strangeness becomes dear,
and chaos familiar, what would I not know and love
of all your world that whispers back in time,
of all this time that images forth a world
to call itself the temporal 'you'!

iii

But the death is here, is now, twines its nightshade
with the first primrose, shines in our music
ironic and ephemeral as the firefly of summer.
The *moritura* is in the discovery, the farewell
is already prepared (with secret tears)
in the first ambiguous greeting, the divided voice
of love-and-death. And all the memories,
the luggage of habit and injury, yours and mine,
the loves, and the half-loves, and the self-loves,
beset us now as once they abetted, divide us now
as once they joined: the four-leafed clover
on the first page of childhood; the cricket
sunning himself on a pebble; the sad rain
on the long windowpanes of illness—you take back these,
as I take back my own. Slow histories recited;
agony projected as sunset on an evening of despair;
friends found and lost; and the dead leaf in the book
to mark the would-be-remembered phrase: all these,
the infinitesimal, or exaggerated, or ridiculous, but cherished:
all these rehearse our death, as if in a ritual
ourselves had prearranged. They reappear to bless us,
and vanish. Even our hatreds bless us and vanish.
Even our self-deceptions, which now, in the moment of sorrow,
we perceive were well-meant, and perhaps even angelic:
the desire to grow, to excel, to see ourselves in a mirror
of godlike beauty, apocalyptic power and wisdom:
even these avert their faces with a sly smile of blessing
and give us back to truth.

95

And the division, the separation, the first dreadful steps
towards separation and division,
oh, these too we must compose into a figure, a foreseen improvisation:
the valedictions transposed into the music,
but as if backward, as if the *aria da capo*
were really conceived at the end, and then cast back.
Scarcely perceptible, the first ghostly recession!
lighter than flute-song of an overtone,
or the quick choice whether to turn or not turn
the profile on a heartbeat of pain. And then, in succession,
half willed, half not, the 'half' separations, and the long backward look,
the net of not-yet-abandoned-hope flung softly out into the abyss,
but withdrawn again, unnoticed, untouched. And so, at last,
long since foreknown and endured, the dread chasm
of the separation itself—

                             whether discovered through the eyes,
which can never have enough of darkness,
or the hands, which would again become inviolable,
or the voices, which would again be still—

all these, already, we have known it from the beginning,
are the conceived and developed and concluded theme,
from signature to coda, of ourselves.
Dear stranger, our love was the music,
we held it for an instant in a handclasp of sunlight,
it is gone, and ourselves gone with it,
the best of us was there, died there.

THE LOVERS

This painful love dissect to the last shred:
abjure it, it will not be solved in bed:
agony of the senses, but compounded
of soul's dream, heart's wish, blood's will, all confounded
with hate, despair, distrust, the fear of each
for what the other brings of alien speech.
Self-love, my love, no farther goes than this,
that when we kiss, it is ourselves we kiss.

O eyes no eyes, but fountains fraught with tears,
o heart no heart, but cistern of the years,
how backward now to childhood's spring we thrust
there to uncover the green shoots of lust:
how forward then to the bare skull we look
to taste our passion dead in doomsday book!
Self-love is all we know, my love, and this
breeds all these worlds, and kills them, when we kiss.

Yet would I give, yet would you take, a time
where self-love were no criminal, no crime:
where the true godhead in each self discovers
that the self-lovers are both gods and lovers.
O love, of this wise love no word be said,
it will be solved in a diviner bed,
where the divine dance teaches self-love this,
that when we kiss it is a god we kiss.

THE CLOVER

The tiger gash of daybreak rips the night
under palmetto leaves drips the first light
the dream is broken the word of water spoken
and the dream bursts with the golden scream
of the unknown bird in the fountained park
hark hark hark screaming beneath blind leaves
and the wild hour is strange and pain strange too
as also too that love to pain should change
the pure love-pattern into deep life-pattern change.
O love, o love, that in the mountains took
this simple heart beside the mountain brook
and broke the golden-rod for summer speech
brimming with water-gold the heart of each,
with what ascending footsteps carved in light
climbing the hyaline we have come to this
animal cry invented in a kiss!
And then the tiger gash of pain
the malicious bird screams in the park again
now at the window screams now at the breast
this breast that lives and loves.

Pray, time, what is our shame
or what this blessedness without a name
that the unknown of love should come to this
animal birth embodied in a kiss?

And this child born in pain of me
the small pale soul that wails in fear of light
what shall I be to him or he to me
now that the dual world is sundered into three?
All's lost in finding, we are swept away
like shoreless mariners, this bed our ship,
nor in this voyage shall we one harbour find,
but separately and alone, love as we may,
seek our own landfall under hostile day.
Farewell, dear voyager—already you depart
who but a moment since lay in my heart.

(And the red leaf turns, turns, in a circle of dust
in the shaft of light that has come and gone
and the light is turning, turning in a ring of darkness
in the mind of night that dreams of waking
and time is turned as sand by the hand is turned
circle in circle ring within ring
till again the finger writes in a circle of dust
in the shaft of light that has come and gone
and the world, my love, comes round
round as the ring of druid oaks in spring
or the ritual hymn the pinkwinks sing,
the world is round as a ring.)

For see, he brings you now his fourleafed clover
who is already (as you bear again) your lover:
and the clear pink-clawed blossoms too,
those that he loves,
clusters that smell like cloves.
As much as you, he loves—as much as you:
and as you turn your head,
on the pale pillow turn your head,
you see the something new
that lights (and listens) in your child, as if
your own eyes there gazed back at you:
and, if with love, yet with a different view.

99

For in that look, that probing interchange,
hovers the thought, perceptible to each,
shines between the eyes, but without speech,
that you surrender now your sovereignty,
but with a kind of acquiescent glee—
you whose thought-wings mount in wider gyre
over the world's wildness, yet know how soon
(time's gift, but also yours)
the child's must always further range, and higher.
This too is a departure, this accolade of clover:
but also, although no mention made,
without a kiss it is conveyed
(although perhaps each wished a kiss)
that now henceforward, far though the voyage take
each on his destined course, the child will keep
your heart, your mind, your love
enringed in his:
your flight, no matter where,
will be ensphered and safely move in his:
no matter, no, how far and faint it soar
or low and lost at last it fall,
his circling love embraces all.
Thus in silence, in the May-morning light,
the mutual accolade.

And o, you guessed, whose generous gesture made
his young thought feel the wing-beat's power
shuddering imagination in that hour
for flaming wheel and falcon tower
over the ruined infernos and gutted heavens
and obliterated purgatories of a world
overwhelmed and overwinged
in range and ring and rise of mind
by feather and ecstasy and blood—

and o, you knew, and meant,
if your own journey went
too early underground
and o poor love for only treason's reason,
too soon, too dark, in the alien spring,
the alien much-loved chinaberry season,
that he would join you there, his vision
flung down with the dust, and the windlost voice
chanting the last verse,
passionately in your grave. For there it stayed,
and there it stays, and there rejoined
to the lost heart, as the slow seasons made
their havoc, from ruin to ruin it too decayed,
fell with you lightly into earth, you two
becoming earth together. But not forgetful,
and not in sleep, if the dust sleeps, is thought to sleep:
for now his life was yours, dedicated to you:

who while he lives will be your lover
(listen, his footstep coming upon the whisper
buena ventura whisper of the Spanish moss)
and brings once more the clear-stemmed clover,
o lost love in this token
sharing with you again, but no word spoken,
that moment's magic, the May-bright morning,
when you evoked so long ago
beyond the chinaberry-shadowed wall
the rings and rituals of your light:
the leaf turning, turning in a circle of dust,
the finger writing, writing, in a ring of dust,
and the mind of night dreaming divine delight:
for the world, my love, comes round,
round as the dance of ancient oaks in spring
or the ritual song the enchanted pinkwinks sing,
the world is round as a ring.

PLAIN SONG

Best come in, the morning's bitter,
pollen float from stars is fatal,
everywhere the abyss lies open,
everywhere laugh dirt and death:

see the descending trap of sunlight
close alike on fly and flower,
membrane into membrane creeping,
vinelike for corruption thrust!

Impure heart that would be single,
multiple soul that would be simple,
watch your daybreak crash in atoms
on the world-coast named despair:

nothing's touched, and nothing's touching:
prey to love, you probe an abscess:
stillness in inebriate motion,
false and fecund fall apart:

even the secret self is faithless,
leers and lies when called to answer:
o divinest, o serenest,
man's invented dream of light!

thousandfold we find its mazes,
more we seek the more it crazes,
best come in, the morning's bitter,
shut the door and wait for night.

EVIL IS THE PALINDROME

Perception is the beginning, sweetheart, perception
opens the window from which we view
terror fluttering toward us down an empty road
delight screaming on dark wings over the hill.
Shall we run? Shall we stand still?
O if we cannot live or love, let us forgive:
evil is the palindrome of live.

The first act is to open our eyes to the light,
the last act is to close them to inward night.
The first act, is it braver than the last,
when we surrender all that is left of us to sleep?
We close our hearts to terror, close them to weep.
If we cannot live or love, let us forgive:
evil is the palindrome of live.

Praise, praise, the dreadful fountain of all blaze,
the immense, cruel, dazzling, spouting source
of ethereal violent living and death-dealing powers:
clouds, sheaved lightnings, burning demonic forms
in angelic and ceaseless creation through the soul's storms.
If we cannot live or love, let us forgive:
evil is the palindrome of live.

Live for the frontier of the daily unknown, of terror,
for the darkness hidden in the striking hand,
the darkness opening in the thinking mind,
the darkness under the valve of the beating heart:
live for the borderland, the daybreak, whence we start
to live and love, and if we cannot live to forgive:
evil is the palindrome of live.

THE ORCHARD

Taking our time by the compass
    our direction by the clock
under the bough, where the windfall
    lies bitten by the frost and the squirrel,
through the jungle, in which imagination
    says 'time has fallen, time is falling,'
the immense jungle of crossed grasses
    and the green celandine of the heart:
who is it that steps like a leaf
    steps and then stops and then steps again
opening the door of cobweb
    to one mortal peril, then another?
who but the whole world in the heart,
    an apple full of seeds, dark seeds,
waiting for the living to be dead,
    and themselves, dead, to be resurrected!

Morning is blue as a child's globe
        on which no map has been drawn:
so, make a windmill of your arms
        and describe a pure circle:
thus the apple tree describes with her boughs
        the fatal fascination of sky,
while, with the same secret design,
        her roots feel the terror of earth.
Nothing divides your footstep
        from the world it rejects and rejoins:
you two are hurrying together
        to the inevitable assignation.
The moon might have been your heart-beat,
        the sun a drop of blood in your hand,
circling forever in the tide
        of the ceaseless know-nothing.

Come, let us square out a space here,
        or have it round like a bird's nest,
a surface to scribble one word upon,
        or a box in which to find keepsakes:
or a room, very small, with one window,
        where sitting we can watch the shadows,
or a bed in which when we wish
        we can make believe that we sleep.
O something we can call our own,
        known and familiar for one moment:
A book that opens at a passage
        of which the meaning is 'maybe':
a face whose eyes have come back
        from the dreadful valley of nightfall:
a face whose eyes cannot stay
        from their holy love of forever.

SUMMER

Absolute zero: the locust sings:
summer's caught in eternity's rings:
the rock explodes, the planet dies,
we shovel up our verities.

The razor rasps across the face
and in the glass our fleeting race
lit by infinity's lightning wink
under the thunder tries to think.

In this frail gourd the granite pours
the timeless howls like all outdoors
the sensuous moment builds a wall
open as wind, no wall at all:

while still obedient to valves and knobs
the vascular jukebox throbs and sobs
expounding hope propounding yearning
proposing love, but never learning

or only learning at zero's gate
like summer's locust the final hate
formless ice on a formless plain
that was and is and comes again.

five

THE CICADA

Views the phenomenal world as a congeries
of shells, casts, and cast-offs, the envelopes
of dead letters, addressees long since lost,
but still of ghostly substance, flung off
and left behind by that which lived and died,
but now, transmuted, leaves in immutable series
the visual equations of essence. It is illusion?
So be it, but it is our veritable speech, our inimitable
shape. Who goes now to the heart
for certainty, the assayable grain of truth?
Fluid and momentary as the auricle's bloodstream.
But in the fossil's curve, limpid in dark rock,
or in the oak's ring, or the king-crab's carapace,
horned for combat long after his wars are done,
yes, and in the mortmain of the printer's page,
still set as the love-song of an antique May,
of which the weather is unrecorded, or, again,
scrolled in the astronomer's sines and symbols, the algebrist's
diminishing abstractions—in these, in these,
O dearest of ephemerids!—in these
how much more permanent is our exchange
whether of love or friendship, the light eye
sounding the unsoundable in the treacherous instant,

than in the summer song, which seems so long, so long,
of the cicada, that brazen jongleur of the trees,
shaking his iridescent rapture!—the subsiding song
spills from the rusted chestnut leaves, is downward lost,
but under the bough still clings, with hooked and feathered claws,
and staring eyes that do not see,
and the split back from which the psyche flew to death,
the crystal chrysalis that will outlast the fall.

What language, this?—The painter's, which is the lover's,
which is the poet's: whose black numbers note
the infinitesimal tick, the monstrous cry.
Grammar and syntax must alike belong
not to the song
but to morphology, the shape that cannot die.

AUBADE

Six o'clock in the crystal instant the crystal second
the crystal pause between systole and diastole
the six glass birds fly one from another
eastward to sunrise out of the sleeping tower
O sleeping man, wake, it is the hour
of crystal meditation, you must compose your death

the six glass birds are flown to the six far corners
where the six columns of crystal uphold the sunrise
but the tower sleeps and the man sleeps
while the wave of sunrise unfolds its volute of prism
O sleeping man, wake, your angel weeps
she who in your slumber dreams to compose your death

six songs it might have been or six devotions
or the six words but not the seventh on the cross
six leaves loosening one and then another
from the praying-tree that waits alone in sunrise
O sleeping man, wake, the hour of loss
opens its crystal heart, you must compose your death

compose your death, O sleeping man, while the six heartbeats
distinct as sandgrains in the hourglass fall
the crystal heartbeats loosening one from another
while the long wave of sunrise unfolds its clouds
O sleeping man, wake, and compose of all
these crystal intricacies of nescience death

of the six words and the six leaves and the six bells
eastward bearing like glass birds the sleeping heart
to the altar of sunrise which the columns uphold
the six crystal columns lucent in sunrise
O sleeping man, wake, it is time to depart,
open your crystal zero, compose your death.

MAYA

We were not seen here before, nor shall be seen
hereafter, nor our garlands of oak-leaves, either;
time was unnoticed, unnumbered, by our empty hands and eyes,
and will be again:

the rain at seven, who had foreseen its elusive silver,
this minuet from dark eaves falling:
or the snow, with its bland deceit over moss and lichen,
or the algebra on the pane:

and the god, too, fallen dejected from his cross, with
      what surprise
to himself and those who loved him:
and all those other gods, of beast and bird and flower,
who died in vain.

Come, let us seek in ourselves, while time includes us,
the illusion's whorled and whirling center;
and praise the imperishable metal of that flower
whose seed was barren grain.

THE ACCOMPLICES

A love I love whose lips I love
but conscience she has none
nor can I rest upon her breast
for faith's to her unknown
light-hearted to my bed she comes
but she is early gone.

This lady in the sunlight is
as magic as the sun
and in my arms and all night long
she seems and is my own
yet but a Monday love is she
and Tuesday she is gone.

Rare as charity is her hand
that rests my heart upon
but charity to so many kind
stays for a day with none
a spendthrift love she spends her love
and all will soon be gone.

Yet though my trust has been betrayed
reproaches have I none
no heart but is of treason made
or has not mischief done
and we could be together false
if she would but stay on.

114

THE MEETING PLACE

The way to meet the unmeetable—? It is this—
to step into the calyx of the sun
at daybreak or a shade before
(for such is the privilege of imagination)
and it will come to you, the event, in some such form
as history requires, though that is not
for immediate consideration. The history
is indeed another and inalterable matter.
For the moment, to meet the moment, you must step forth
fearlessly or with awareness of fear:
and that is perhaps better, for fear
is that by which you live, with which you die,
the edge of death, as it was the edge of birth.
What, pray, does the ailanthus do with its seeds
shaken at three o'clock by the alien southeast
to a shower of snow or is it sleet or a feathery
rainfall of blossom to the unreceptive
stones of a human path? Out of such
and into such unhuman paths we sow
without hope of fruit, maybe, our deeds or deaths
or seeds of hope. But what then
when the ailanthus in the penultimate April
or ultimate and desired May gives up
bloom for leaves, for the last time leaves
bloom for leaves?

                    For then it is, dear tree, dear heart,
dear earth, dear god, and all we love and owned,
when the deciduous becomes tired, that history
begins and speaks. When we no longer dream
forward, but only backward, in the desired May,
and death no longer in the fruit is in the root
then it is that history speaks
and the last sunset is the first, the first
sunrise becomes the last, the tree becomes again the seed,
and in a twinkling is again the tree,
and we are seed and tree, and we
like gods can both remember and forget,
and the unmeetable is met.

THE FLUTEPLAYER

Excellent o excellent in morning sunlight
that slides in planes of water through this tree
O chinaberry tree dedicated to daybreak
as daybreak the unfolding rose is dedicated to thee
but who was in this garden what god was in this garden
breathed here upon his flute before we came
who was here of whom we do not know the name

light slides its crystal over silent leaves
crystal delight for thee blest chinaberry tree
but who was he who in this garden
blew on his flute the two-voiced myth
before we came
sounding in changing shapes and guises
his two-voiced name

for there was someone here someone unknown
of whom these shapes and colors speak
someone O chinaberry tree who speaks in thee
on the path this side of night
speaks still in shade or substance the lost name
he left behind, the absent-minded god
who blew his two-voiced flute before we came.

HERMAN MELVILLE

'My towers at last!'—

                      What meant the words
from what acknowledged circuit sprung
and in the heart and on the tongue
at sight of few familiar birds
when seaward his last sail unfurled
to leeward from the wheel once more
bloomed the pale crags of haunted shore
that once-more-visited notch of world:
and straight he knew as known before
the Logos in Leviathan's roar
he deepest sounding with his lead
who all had fathomed all had said.

Much-loving hero—towers indeed
were those that overhung your log
with entries of typhoon and fog
and thunderstone for Adam's breed:
man's warm Sargasso Sea of faith
dislimned in light by luck or fate
you for mankind set sail by hate
and weathered it, and with it death.
And now at world's end coasting late
in dolphined calms beyond the gate
which Hercules flung down, you come
to the grim rocks that nod you home.

Depth below depth this love of man:
among unnumbered and unknown
to mark and make his cryptic own
one landfall of all time began:
of all life's hurts to treasure one
and hug it to the wounded breast,
in this to dedicate the rest,
all injuries received or done.
Your towers again but towers now blest
your haven in a shoreless west
O mariner of the human soul
who in the landmark notched the Pole
and in the Item loved the Whole.

WHEN YOU ARE NOT SURPRISED

When you are not surprised, not surprised,
nor leap in imagination from sunlight into shadow
or from shadow into sunlight
suiting the color of fright or delight
to the bewildering circumstance
when you are no longer surprised
by the quiet or fury of daybreak
the stormy uprush of the sun's rage
over the edges of torn trees
torrents of living and dying flung
upward and outward inward and downward to space
or else
peace peace peace peace
the wood-thrush speaking his holy holy
far hidden in the forest of the mind
while slowly
the limbs of light unwind
and the world's surface dreams again of night
as the center dreams of light

when you are not surprised
by breath and breath and breath
the first unconscious morning breath
the tap of the bird's beak on the pane
and do not cry out come again
blest blest that you are come again
o light o sound o voice of bird o light
and memory too o memory blest
and curst with the debts of yesterday
that would not stay, or stay

when you are not surprised
by death and death and death
death of the bee in the daffodil
death of color in the child's cheek
on the young mother's breast
death of sense of touch of sight
death of delight
and the inward death the inward turning night
when the heart hardens itself with hate and indifference
for hated self and beloved not-self
when you are not surprised
by wheel's turn or turn of season
the winged and orbèd chariot tilt of time
the halcyon pause, the blue caesura of spring
and solar rhyme
woven into the divinely remembered nest
by the dark-eyed love in the oriole's breast
and the tides of space that ring the heart
while still, while still, the wave of the invisible world
breaks into consciousness in the mind of god
then welcome death and be by death benignly welcomed
and join again in the ceaseless know-nothing
from which you awoke to the first surprise.

PORTRAIT

Seven-starred eyes beneath the seven-starred mind
young Helen's eyes with flaming Troy behind
and in the labyrinths of fatal hair
the dying Minotaur and Theseus on the stair

and as I drink the thieving Argonauts
sail from this table with our ravished thoughts
to trade our love the honey of Hybla bees
beyond the sunset rocks the knees of Hercules.

Arcane immortal shameless is that face
rich with the present timelessness of race
the ageless smile for me but also still
the secret smile of triumph for Samson at the mill—

dead kings dead heroes nailed like stars above
in the cold constellations of her love
none there forgotten none who desired escape
and we, we too, alas, must in that myth take shape.

THE FOUNTAIN

In the evening we heard the dead leaves
skittering away over asphalt
in the morning saw a sequin of sunlight
slotted through a crack in the wall
bright gold on the woodshed floor
but no it did not tremble it was only
the pale yellow leaf of the locust.

And look now the golden-eyed tree-toad
flips through a thicket of shadow
to breathe by the sodden bird's nest
the goldfinch caught in a ring of light
taps at the eaves and Sheepfold Hill
once more wears its Joseph's coat colors
while wild geese honk at the tideline.

Voices of death voices of creation
for the blonde rondure of the full moon
and the bat's dizzy sky-skatings
we light now the first candle
sheltered between tender-bright palms
for a secret instant of self.

Now phrase be praise and praise be phrase
for the brook with a stone in its path
the man with no thought in his mind
the girl with no love in her heart
the shooting star lost in a vapor
and the wind stilled at sunset.

Caught with these in a moment of silence
we become one instant of the forever-together
the fountain of god-speech motionless in falling
action spellbound in the moment of meaning
words and worlds still enough at last to be counted
if only there was someone to count them.

CREPE MYRTLE
F.D.R.: APRIL 12, 1945

i

Leaves, and waves, and years. Shadows of leaves, shadows of
waves, and shadows of years.
What will the boy recall of them
himself a leaf hurrying among leaves
planking of a lost whaler adrift among waves
washed and aspersed to the tolling of the years, until at length
the man remembers the boy, the man
drawing nostalgic pictures of the past with a stick?
'What have I seen? The leaves blown in harsh waves
waves scattered like leaves to leeward blown
leeward from the brave foolish heart, the intrepid mind,
but to be summoned again in a moment of vision
by waves no mind can control.'
Landward charge the white horses everlastingly
from the blinding notch of the sea-rim, numberless, calling
and falling, lapsing and collapsing, each at last
to become in substance one with another
or in motion with one and in substance with all:
seaward the charioteers the white manes riding
from the known shore to the unknown shoreless faring,
beyond the remembering vision of him who beholds
once for an instant the beginning of the endless.
Waves of leaves, waves of waves, waves of years:
but the sound at last silent, less than the chuckle
of the falling fountain of thought, the motion becoming
the symbol, only, of motion,
and simplified at last, and still.

ii

But look: the record of a handful of leaves
dances on the moonlit wall of an old house, opens
silent fingers, closes them again, points quickly,
and then is replaced by nothing, without comment
the slide removed from the magic lantern.
Perhaps to return again, altered, in sunlight, or yet again
to be altered anew, unrecognized, in leafless winter.
O blind dark darkness of self, blind dark brightness
of the surely not implacable, not unknowable, Other!
wave of the outer forever falling into the wave of the inner!
can we decipher here behind the quick shutter
in the single tremor of insight
the final meaning of shadow? The crepe myrtle
disowns its shadow on hard earth faded with blossom
designs a cemetery wall with echo of bloom
signals a moving message over the headstone, sliding
its cryptic stencil, life-and-death, between
old earth and new moon.

                        As here! reshaping
in the spring night! the lantern hung among tombs,
the pick striking a spark from granite, the spade
divulging the loose sub-tropic humus, the past!
and the old vault lies open,
empty to the fetid and aromatic night,
empty of all save the soft and silken dust,
dust as fine as hair or as passion, elusive
as moonlight on the shell road: empty of all
save a single gleam in the corner by the red wall:
and quickly as a heartbeat or cry unearthed,
shining again for the lantern after a hundred years,
the silver sword-hilt, the rusted sword-blade.

And behold, the hero walks again among men,
the living dead man salutes the dead men who still live,
and they stiffen, hearing the lost bugle of Eutaw Springs
across the cypress swamp in the dead of winter:
the voice of wisdom that trembles from the ground,
the voice of honour that trembles in rusted steel.

iii

The coffin of the great man travels slowly
through the applause of silence the applause of flags
the applause of tears and empty hearts, the applause
of the last and greatest loneliness, the speechless
loneliness of the great vision: the coffin of the great man
travels slowly over earth, slowly under sky,
slowly through the sun-sequined shadow, slowly through
    the shade,
slowly under the evening star and the faint new moon
and again now into the pre-dawn silence, and the first
pinewood voice of the mocking-bird, while eastward
under the Pole Star leans the world to the light
and the light falls on the pine-barrens like moss roses
and on the mountains like smoke. The coffin of the great man
travels under the arch of time without pausing
and without pausing under the arch of eternity
and without pausing under the arch of the infinite
travelling now as the earth travels, joining the earth,
turning to the right with the earth as it faces the Pole Star
they two becoming in substance one with another
in motion at one and in substance with all.
The coffin of the great man travels slowly
slowly and well through the seasons, the spring passing
over into the rich summer, and with the earth
revolves under the changing arch of the years.

And now the avenues of weeping are still, the applause
of silence itself is hushed, and the empty hearts
are again refilled with love, the limp flags
stiffen anew at the masthead. And it is he,
himself, the great man dead, who teaches us,
speaking from the coffin, already empty, and the grave
empty also. For the greatness is not there,
travelled not slowly thither with the slow coffin,
slowly to turn with earth under time's arch,
but is given to us to keep. The great man's name
walks again among us, the living greatness
speaks in ourselves. And we hear him saying
—as we heard the bugle of Eutaw Springs
sing in a sword-blade—'Finis coronat opus—
death crowns the work, not the man!' The voice of wisdom
trembling in our own hearts, the voice of honour
trembling in the broken sword.

                             Leaves, and waves, and years:
shadow of a handful of leaves that dances
on the wall of an empty house, the crepe myrtle
designing a cemetery wall with echo of bloom,
signalling a message over the headstone, sliding
her cryptic stencil, life-and-death between
the old earth and new moon. And in our minds, now his,
where the waves are falling, falling, each at last
to become in substance one with another
or in motion with one and in substance with all,
seaward the charioteers the white manes riding
from the known shore to the unknown shoreless fare:
beyond the remembering vision of him who beheld
once and forever the beginning of the endless.

THE CYCLADS

They have been no longer than usual in arriving at this place.
Terror of time, they murmur, equals the terror of space.
All cancels out in the end, they say, and the end is nothing.
And all between a nothing in borrowed clothing.
Here we have stars—even of the first magnitude—
how flattering these human terms!—doomed to decrepitude,
all things, even the little atom, in its slow dying, arrive here,
and then slip silently x-ward to a predestined year.
Who would plant trees here? Is it an honest man?
As if to shade coming chaos in his wistful plan?
God knows, not we. At least, we plant no tree.
We only wait in the Absolute and see.

Yes, Old Repetition, they have been no longer than usual:
only to itself, perhaps, does time's cycle seem casual:
and space, this horrid cloaca which we must share,
finds no mirror in which to face its face in when or where.
Not in us surely? But perhaps in these, who seem
the endless repetition of our dream:
cold algebra brought round once more in a concentric hell:
convolute whirlwind in an invisible shell.
How vast, how still, how slow! We sleep and, wake, and then,
cloud-walking, watch our dream pour past again.

129

They have been no longer than usual, this time, in coming.
Behold the shadows of spokes, the wheels are humming,
street-lights and neon monsters glare on the cloud,
from violet dynamos, an endless belt, spills out the crowd.
And all at once. Dim past, dim future, all at once:
the moral histories, the cracked applause, the festered battlefronts:
the corner drug-store where the lyric cash-tray sings:
and the amateur astronomer peering at Saturn's rings.
But this is not all, by no means, no! This is not all.
No, choose your own show, midway or sideshow: from Adam's Fall
to ill-starred Lucifer, and the blind poet's dictated dream:
O purblind doomed panhandler of the siltage in time's stream.